An Introduction to

Text and Discourse Analysis

An Introduction to

Text and Discourse Analysis

IAN POPLE

Investigating English Language

STANLEY THORNES (PUBLISHERS) LTD

First published in 1998 by:
Stanley Thornes (Publishers) Ltd
Ellenborough House
Wellington Street
CHELTENHAM GL50 1YW
England

98 99 00 01 02 / 10 9 8 7 6 5 4 3 2 1

A catalogue record for this book is available from the British Library.

ISBN 0-7487-3357-4

Typeset by Tech-Set Ltd, Gateshead, Tyne & Wear
Printed and bound in Great Britain by Scotprint Ltd., Musselburgh, Scotland

CONTENTS

5 Looking at conversation

Acknowledgements

Author's note

Thanks are due to Eliška Kedlesková, James Fahy, Thomas Bloor and Keith Richards for their contributions to Chapter 5.

Particular thanks are due to Geoff Palmer, whose immaculate copy editing turned my manuscript into a much better book than was originally delivered.

The author and publishers wish to thank the following for permission to use copyright material:

Bliss magazine for material from 'Face to Face Therapy', *Bliss*, August 1996; Bloodaxe Books for Simon Armitage, 'Very Simply Topping up the Brake Fluid' from *Zoom*, 1989; Boosey & Hawkes Music Publishers Ltd for an excerpt from 'These Foolish Things' by Jack Strachey/Eric Maschwitz. Copyright © 1932 Lafleur Music Ltd; Cobuild Ltd for definitions from *Collins* COBUILD *English Language Dictionary* and *Collins* COBUILD *English Grammar*; The Economist for material from 'Dinosaur dentist detective', *The Economist*, 24.8.96. Copyright © The Economist 1996; and 'Matrix for a modern monarchy', *The Economist*, 24.8.96. Copyright © The Economist 1996; English & Media Centre for material from Jane Ogborn, 'In the wake of Dearing Post 16', *The English & Media Magazine*, 36, Summer 1997; Guardian Media Group plc for material from various issues of *The Guardian* and *The Observer*; The Hargreaves Organisation for material from *Mr Bounce, Mr Noisy, Mr Busy, Mr Skinny, Mr Small, Mr Sneeze and Mr Mischief* by Roger Hargreaves. Copyright © by Mrs Roger Hargreaves; Tony Harrison for an excerpt from 'V' from *Selected Poems*, Penguin Books, 1987; Helicon Publishing Ltd for definitions, 'The Beatles' and 'Bluestocking' from *Hutchinson Encyclopedia*. Copyright © Helicon Publishing 1997; The Controller of her Majesty's Stationery Office for material from 'Family Expenditure Survey' In *Britain 1994: An Official Handbook*, Fig. 1. Crown copyright; David Higham Associates on behalf of the author for material from Richard Hughes, *In Hazard*, Chatto & Windus, 1938; International Music Publications Ltd for an excerpt from 'My Favourite Things' by Rodgers/Hammerstein II, Williamson Music, owner of publication and Allied Rights throughout the world. Copyright © 1959 by Richard Rogers & Oscar Hammerstein; Ewan MacNaughton Associates on behalf of Telegraph Group Ltd for 'The Pursuit of Youth' from Suzi Robinson, *The Book of Mini Sagas*, 1985. Copyright © Telegraph Group Ltd 1985; and material from Caroline Davies, 'Rat Boy, *The Daily Telegraph*, 3.4.97. Copyright © Telegraph Group Ltd 1997; Suniti Namjoshi for 'The Oyster Child' from *Feminist Fables*, Virago, 1994; Newspaper Publishing plc for material from Patrick Cockburn, 'Kurds eke a living', *Independent on Sunday*, 20.10.96; News International Associated Services Ltd for material from Olga Craig, 'Hermit boy is rescued from home of squalor', *Today*, 27.11.91; W W Norton & Company for E E Cummings, 'she being Brand' from *Complete Poems 1904-1962*, ed. George Firmage. Copyright © 1991 by the Trustees for the E E Cummings Trust and George James Firmage; Oxford University Press or material from J McH Sinclair and R M Coulthard, *Towards an Analysis of Discourse*. Copyright © Oxford University Press 1975; Penguin UK for an extract from Donna Tartt, *The Secret History*, Viking Penguin, 1992 pp. 201-3. Copyright © Donna Tartt 1992; BBC Worldwide for material from *Radio Times*, June 28th – 4th July 1997; Scottish Amicable for material from Personal Pension document Y720/1/96; Sugar Magazine for material from *Sugar*, 24, October 1996; Woman magazine for front cover of *Woman*, 17th April 1995.

Every effort has been made to trace all the copyright holders, but if any have been inadvertently overlooked the publishers will be pleased to make the necessary arrangements at the first opportunity.

Introduction

This book is intended to introduce you to some methods of looking at the way in which language – in this case the English language – is held together. It suggests that written language and spoken language have certain patterns, and that it is these patterns that hold language together. My use of the word 'text' applies to both written and spoken language. The word 'discourse' applies not only to the product; that is, the final 'text' that we see written down, or that we hear being spoken. It also applies to the process by which we arrive at that final text. 'Discourse analysis' sees the process out of which the text evolves as being very important.

Grammar is another important way in which language is held together and is an important part of what we will examine in this book. However, you will be looking at stretches of language larger than single sentences. To examine texts larger than single sentences, you cannot just use the tools of grammar. The rules of grammar show us how to combine words so that those words make acceptable sentences. Unfortunately, grammar alone cannot tell us how we can fit sentences together to make longer stretches of text. This is where text and discourse analysis comes in.

Text and discourse analysis is a way of examining the ways in which sentences and even longer stretches of language fit together. In Chapter 1, you will be introduced to the idea of 'text' and what makes a text. You will see how easily a text can break down. At the same time, you will see how strong the forces are which hold text together.

In Chapter 2, you will look at the way in which grammar plays its part in combining sentences so that they fit together in an acceptable way.

In Chapter 3, you will see how words and their meanings form certain patterns that affect the way in which texts 'cohere', and the ways in which the meanings of words combine to create coherence in texts. In this chapter, we will also examine the way in which that coherence is affected by the context in which it happens – the social area in which the text works.

In Chapter 4, we will examine patterns of larger stretches of written language. These often cohere because of the functions performed by those pieces of text. Those functions, in turn, affect the way in which sentences, and sometimes paragraphs, combine.

Finally, in Chapter 5, we will look at spoken language, demonstrating that spoken language can be organised by the speakers at the time of speaking. In the final section of the chapter, we will examine the way in which speech is organised in particular situations.

This book is highly interactive. This means that there are many questions for the reader to try to answer. It is important that you, the reader, think in depth about the way in which sentences and spoken utterances combine. This will help you to think about the language that you meet when you close this book and put it down. In addition, there are many activities for you to try out. There are writing activities, in which you will take the techniques that you have studied in the book and use them to create coherent texts of your own. We hope this will show you how the processes of discourse are operating in every text that you come across. This is why there is a wide variety of texts to illustrate the points being made. You will examine texts ranging from jokes and verses of songs, to instructions for fitting lights to bikes, and passages from the Mr Men books. All of these texts are made coherent by the processes of discourse.

This book is not intended to be read straight through, although it would be possible to do that. It is essentially a work book, a resource to be used at points in a course at which the need arises. As such, it is aimed at students and teachers working towards the Advanced and Advanced Supplementary courses in English Language. It may also prove useful for students beginning undergraduate courses in English Language and Literature.

Throughout the text, important terms are highlighted in **bold** type. Those terms that are printed in **<u>bold underlined</u>** type are described in more detail in the Glossary at the end of the volume.

1 What is text?

1.0 Introduction

It is not always easy to answer the question 'What is **text**?'. You may like to think of a text as a collection of words. You may change that definition to make sure that a text is a collection of words in the correct order. But what is 'the correct order' and who decides what the correct order is? The whole point of this book to help you to think about this. This chapter is to help you start that process.

1.1 Identifying text

First, I would like you to answer one or two questions:

▷ Is the following a text?

Added	and	bank	being
excitement	left	miscalculating	of
on	wrong	the	the
there's	tide	times	stranded

[Gordon Burn, *Alma Cogan*, Minerva, 1992]

▷ If it isn't a text, can you make it into a text?
▷ If you have now made it into a text, what did you do to make it into a text?
▷ And what can you call what you have made?

If you have made it into a text, you will have used the 'forces' of **grammar** to create the text. You will know that

'the' + 'adjective' + 'noun' = 'phrase'

so you will have ended up with *the added excitement* and *the wrong bank*. You will also know that *excitement* is often followed by *of*. And you will have worked through the rest of the words until you have put them into the 'right' order; or put them into an order that 'makes sense'. (There are a number of different ways of ordering the words.)

I've used the word 'know' a number of times here. You don't have to 'know' in conscious, active terms that

'the' [definite article] + 'adjective' + 'noun' = 'phrase'

but you do know unconsciously and intuitively.

▷ Is the following a text – and if it isn't a text, why isn't it?

through the Mmmmmmmmmmmmm-Mateson's bacon wrappers	on the way	it's a short walk
and the dog gets the chance	to the crossing point	across the rocks and seaweed
to unload a couple of doo-doo's	and spaghetti hoop cans	and washed up tumble driers

[Gordon Burn, op. cit.]

If you put this into 'the right order', what did you have at the end? You probably had several different versions. That's because it wasn't only the 'forces of grammar' that helped you. You were also dealing with something called **syntax**. Syntax is grammar, but it also has to do with the more general ways in which we put words and **phrases** into the 'right order'. We could also describe the 'forces of syntax', or the reasons why you chose to put certain phrases in certain places. But, here again, we don't have to. You knew intuitively where things went.

Now do the same with these groups of sentences:

1	'It's another one of my experiments. To see how I look best. So when the time comes I'll be ready.' She opened a lipstick and painted on a bright pink mouth.
2	'It's important to experiment, so when the time comes you're all ready. I'm going to be a kisser some day. Want to see something else?'
3	Nancy studied herself in the heartshaped mirror. She rubbed her lips together. 'Well, maybe you're right.' She wiped off the lipstick with a tissue. 'My mother would kill me if I came out like this anyway.'
4	'I practice a lot though,' Nancy said. 'Practice what?' I asked. 'Kissing! Isn't that what we were talking about? Kissing!
5	I looked. There were a million little bottles, jars and tubes. There were more cosmetics in that drawer than my mother had all together. I asked, 'What do you do with all that stuff?'
6	'How can you practice that? I asked. 'Watch this.' Nancy grabbed her pillow and embraced it. She gave it a long kiss. When she was done she threw the pillow on the bed.
7	I just stood there with my mouth half open. Nancy sat down at her dressing table and opened a drawer. 'Look at this,' she said.
8	'Well, what do you think?' 'Umm … I don't know. It's kind of bright, isn't it?'

[Judy Blume, *Are You There God? It's Me, Margaret*, Victor Gollancz, 1979]

▷ How easy was it to turn that into a text?
▷ How many 'correct' or sensible versions of the final text can you have? There is more than one.

1.2 Coherence

The fact that you are able to put these sentences into a 'correct' order is at the heart of everything in this book. In the same way as you have intuitive ideas about grammar and syntax, you also have intuitive ideas about the right order of stretches of language that are larger than the sentence. You have intuitive ideas about what makes a text **coherent**. Before you put groups **1–8** into a 'correct order', the text was incoherent. In the same way that we might talk about the forces of grammar, we can also talk about the 'forces of coherence'. Those are the forces that create the process of **coherence**. Some people have suggested that the process of putting together is **discourse**. The final product after you have finished putting things together is the **text**.

Let's look at this from another point of view:

▷ What is the matter with the following text?

> *There is a cat on the lawn. The lawn needs mowing. My kids have lots of needs. The next door neighbour's goat has kids. My Dad has kid skin gloves.*

We can see that all these sentences are related. There is a word in each sentence that is the same as one used in the previous sentence. Sometimes the meaning of the word has changed between sentences, but the word itself hasn't – for example, *kids* meaning *children* and *kids* meaning *baby goats*.

We can see here that there is a kind of **cohesion** to the text – it sticks together. But it doesn't have any meaning. It isn't coherent.

Now look at another example:

▷ Is it a text? Does it have stick together in the way in which you have made the previous texts stick together? Does it have a coherent meaning?

> *Chris: Hello Jozef.*
> *Jozef: Hello Chris … Could you do me a great favour.*
> *Chris: Yeah.*
> *Jozef: I'm going to book four cinema tickets on the phone and they need a credit card number … could you give me your credit card number … they only accept payment by credit card over the phone.*
> *Chris: Ah,*
> *Jozef: I telephoned there and they said they wouldn't do any reservations*
> *Chris: without a card.*
> *Jozef: Yes and I could pay you back in cash.*
> *Chris: Yes … sure … no problem at all.*
>
> [Michael McCarthy, *Discourse Analysis for Language Teachers*, Cambridge University Press, 1991]

I think that you'll agree that this text seems to stick together in the way in which you have been able to make most of the previous texts stick together. You know, for example, who *you* and *I* refer to in the text. But who does *they* refer to in Jozef's second speech? You can't refer back in the text to find exactly who *they* refers to. But we can certainly make valid suggestions.

▷ Does the text have coherent meaning?
▷ What kinds of patterns we can find in the conversation? For example, are there any questions and answers in the conversations?
▷ Is there a question that isn't answered until later in the conversation?
▷ Chris makes a number of very short comments. What jobs do these answers perform?
▷ When you think about all of these, you can see that there is a pattern to the conversation. But is it a text?

Because it is written down, we can call it a text. One of the most important parts of looking at language is to look at **conversation** – and one of the most important ways of looking at conversation is to write it down and look at the way in which it can form into patterns. We will be looking at this in greater detail in Chapter 5. But before we do that …

▷ What are the main differences between the piece of conversation in this chapter and the texts taken from books?

WRITING ACTIVITY A

1 Try to write an incoherent text like that on page 5. Exchange your version with that of someone else. Can the other person make your text more cohesive and less incoherent?

2 Invent names for two people. Write down everything you can imagine about those two people and their lives; for example, what kind of house they live in, what jobs they do, what they watch on TV, which sports they like and which teams they support. Think about the small details of their lives – which brand of toothpaste they use, what they think about when they do the washing up, how brown they like their toast, and so on. Now write down a **dialogue** between these two people. How like the 'real' conversation on page 5 is your dialogue? Can you work out the ways in which it is like the conversation and the ways in which it isn't?

2 Grammatical cohesion

2.0 Introduction

In this chapter, you will be looking at the way in which grammar helps to make a text coherent. In particular, you will be looking at the way in which there are words whose usual meaning is only concerned with making text coherent.

2.1 Reference

Look at these sentences:

> *General Jumbo arrived at the office wearing a new uniform made of New Zealand material. He is delighted with it and turned round very slowly to show it to me, keeping his feet in a v like a small boy at a dancing class. He looked a like a giant teddy bear.*
>
> [Hermione, Countess of Ranfurly, *To War with Whitaker: the Wartime Diaries of the Countess of Ranfurly*, Heinemann, 1994]

▷ Who do the words *he* and *his* refer to, and what does the word *it* refer to?
▷ Who do you think *me* is, and where is *me*: in the passage or outside it?

Note how the phrase 'refer to' is used. One of the clearest ways in which text is bound together is through the use of <u>**reference**</u>. Reference is created through the use of a specific number of items:

- **Personal pronouns** (*I, me, you, she, he, it, her, him, we, us, they, them*) – for example:

  He borrowed the money from them.

- **Possessives** (*mine, yours, hers, his, its, ours, theirs*) – for example:

  That book is mine.

- Possessive adjectives (*my, your, her, his, our, their*) – for example:

  His horse came in last at Kempton.

We can call this <u>**personal reference**</u>.

- **Demonstratives** (*this/these, that/those, here/there, now/then*) – for example:

  Lieutenant Hassab wants to see me at 12 o'clock, but I don't think I can see him then.

- **Comparatives** (*the same as, bigger than, identical to, fewer than*, and so on) – for example:

  Television viewers were urged yesterday to store their sets in the coldest and most uncomfortable room in their homes at the start of Turn Off TV week.

                                                          [*The Times*, 25 April 1997]

It is important to note that these are words that do not have a complete meaning by themselves. To find that meaning we have to refer to something else; we refer back in the text, forward in the text, or out of the text itself, to the context or situation of the text.

2.1.1 Text reference: pronouns

There are two main jobs for pronouns and comparatives. The first job is to refer to things in the text that we are reading; we can call this **text reference**. There are two main types of text reference. First, we can refer back to an earlier part of the text, as you did at the beginning of this section – or as in this next example, taken from a text in Chapter 1:

  Nancy grabbed her pillow and embraced it. She gave it a long kiss.

The pronoun *it* refers back to the word *pillow* in the previous sentence. When words refer backwards in a text, we can call that **anaphoric reference**.

ACTIVITY 1

1 Find the pronouns in the following short passage and draw a circle round them. Then draw a line from the pronoun to the thing that it refers to. Some have been done for you.

2 Look at the two uses of this in the passage. What is different about them, and how are they different from the personal pronouns and the possessive adjective that occur in the passage?

  Police were on the boat, talking to Captain Ma. An officer came up to Mr T'Chung and fired a string of questions at (him.)
    'People's police will come to hotel this evening,' said Mr T'Chung.
    All this would normally have interested Wexford very much. The reason (it) didn't was that (he) had been aware, all the way down the hill, of the old woman with the bound feet following him at a distance. He turned round once or twice, like Shelley's traveller, he told himself, and saw not exactly a frightful fiend but this old creature, hobbling on her stick, who was becoming fiendish enough to him. Now about to enter the bus, the heat thick and gleaming, radiated off the still blue water in a dazzling glare, he made himself turn round and face behind her boldly. She was gone. There was nowhere for her to disappear to but she was gone.
                                          [Ruth Rendell, *The Speaker of Mandarin*, Arrow, 1983]

Now look at the pronoun *I* in the following passage:

> *It is probably the most dangerous way to make a living in the world. 'I do it because I would prefer to die than see the rest of my family starve,' said Sabir Saleh, a middle-aged man who used to be a farmer but is now too poor to hire a tractor to plough his land.*

[*Independent on Sunday*, 20 October 1996]

The *I* refers forwards to the name *Sabir Saleh*. When a pronoun refers forwards, we say that it is **cataphoric** (remember that 'cats walk forwards').

We can see this in those rather contrived essays that children write when they are asked to write about one of their pets:

> *She was fierce and dark in the night. Her eyes looked menacingly on everything she saw. Her teeth glinted sharply and her claws curved to sharp points. She strode smoothly and powerfully down the path. She was mistress of all she surveyed. My cat Fluffy was on patrol for mice and other creatures.*

You can see that *she* and *her* refer forwards to *My cat Fluffy* in the last sentence. *She* is described in terms of power and aggression. However, the cat has a very innocent name. That contrast is made possible because the cataphoric *she* withholds information until you find out who or what *she* is.

The use of cataphoric reference is often present on the covers of magazines. Look at this cover (shown on page 10) and then decide what the pronouns and possessive adjectives refer to:

a Our baby
b Our house
c Between 'us'
d My beauty secrets
e I love my new hairstyle

▷ Why do you think this kind of reference is used on the front cover of magazines?

ACTIVITY 2

Put together a collection of magazine covers. Which magazines use the type of cataphoric referencing that you have just read about? Group the magazines into those that do use this type of referencing and those that do not. What are the differences between the magazines that do use such referencing and those that do not? Does this tell you anything about the readers of the different types of magazines?

This kind of cataphoric reference is also often used at the beginning of newspaper and magazine articles. Look at the following beginnings:

▷ What do the possessive adjective *His* at the beginning of the first extract and the pronoun *It* at the beginning of the second extract actually refer to?
▷ What effects are gained by using cataphoric references in journalistic texts such as these?

1 *His nickname came to epitomise the menace of the under-age criminal. It was inspired by his choice of hideaways – the warm ventilation ducts on his council estate while on the run. He was constantly being hunted by the police for the burglaries he carried out to fund his glue-sniffing habit.*

  He needed a nickname because as a juvenile he could not be identified by the media. But this week, four years after he first gained notoriety as a 13-year-old persistent offender, 'Rat Boy' has been publicly named as Anthony Kennedy, aged 17.

[*The Daily Telegraph*, 3 April 1997]

2 *It has been remarkably durable. While similar operations folded in Russia, Gemany and most of the rest of Europe over the past two centuries, the House of Windsor has proved its ability to adapt again and again to changing customer demand. Yet the past ten years have been as tough as any since the late 18th century, when the chief executive lost his marbles as well as one of the company's principal assets, America.*

[*The Economist*, vol. 340, no. 7980, 24 August 1996]

Look at the first pronoun *It* in the next passage, which is a continuation of a text that you looked at above:

▷ Because *It* is the first word in the text, we can assume that it does refer forward, but does it refer to any words that are actually in the text? Or does it refer to an idea in the text?
▷ Can you sum that idea up in two words?

  It is probably the most dangerous way to make a living in the world. 'I do it because I would prefer to die than see the rest of my family starve,' said Sabir Saleh, a middle-aged man who used to be a farmer but is now too poor to hire a tractor to plough his land.

  Every morning he goes out into the minefields laid around Penjwin, a village in northern Iraq shattered by fighting in the Iran–Iraq war. Mr Saleh looks for one mine in particular: the Italian made Valmara, one of the most lethal anti-personnel mines in existence. …

  'I defuse the mine with a piece of wire,' said Mr Saleh. 'Then I unscrew the top of it and take out the aluminium around the explosives. When I have taken apart six mines I have enough aluminium to sell for 30 dinar (about 75 pence) to a shop in Penjwin.' After a day in the minefields he hopes to have recovered enough aluminium to feed his family of eight.

[*Independent on Sunday*, 20 October 1996]

We could suggest that *it* refers to something like *mine clearing* or *mine defusing*. We can see that neither of those phrases actually appears in the passage, but we get the idea of mine clearing or defusing from the passage. So *it* can refer to an 'idea' or a 'fact' that is present in the passage.

What effect does the writer gain from using a cataphoric *it* at the beginning of the passage, and what effect is gained by *it* not actually referring to particular words? In the first case, we can suggest that the writer gains an element of suspense. You, the reader, read on/forward because you want to find out what the *it* refers to. In the second case, the writer may make you read more intently to emphasise the danger of what the man does, of why he does it, and on what he and his family stand to lose if he doesn't do the work.

▷ Why do you think that the writer has not written *Mine clearing is probably the most dangerous way to make a living in the world*?

ACTIVITY 3

Read the following passage. Circle the pronouns in it and draw lines from the pronouns to the things that they refer to:

> *Pym closed the curtains and put the lights back on. I will make my own daytime and my own night. The briefcase stood where he had left it, strangely rigid from its steel lining. Everybody carried cases, he remembered, as he stared at it. Rick's was pigskin, Lippsie's was cardboard, Poppy's was a scruffy grey thing with marks printed on it to look like hide. And Jack – dear Jack – you have your marvellous old attaché case, faithful as the dog you had to shoot.*

[John Le Carré, A Perfect Spy, Coronet, 1986]

2.1.2 Situation reference

We have just seen that it is usually possible to draw the connection between a pronoun and the thing that it refers to, or its **referent**. Another job for a pronoun is to refer to things outside the text that we are reading, usually to the situation of that text – the world around it. This is also known as **exophoric** reference. Strictly speaking, **situation reference** does not help to bind a text or make it more 'cohesive'. If the pronoun refers to something outside the piece that we are reading, then we can't usually say that the pronoun refers to anything that we have read or are about to read. However, we will look at situation reference because it has important – but sometimes difficult – effects upon a text.

We can see situation reference most clearly in conversation. If we look at the following conversation between a doctor and two students in a hospital, we can see that the *he* is clearly the patient. But the patient is not actually in the text – the patient doesn't say anything. We can't draw a neat little line from the *he* to its referent in the text:

> A: … what's he look like does he look well.
> B: he looks fairly well but then we've had a sunny Easter (LAUGHTER)
> A: yes but does he look as if he's lost an awful lot of weight that he's suffered loss of sleep due to pain general things
> C: he looks a little bit thin but doesn't look a particularly er worried sort of man
> A: no he looks fairly fit doesn't he
> C: fairly fit

The *he* refers outside the text, the words, the conversation: it refers to the poor patient lying on his bed, who is being talked about in this way.

Now read the following poem by the American poet, e. e. cummings. As you read it, locate the personal pronouns and possessive adjectives; use the line numbering to help you do this.

▷ What do the pronouns refer to?
▷ Where is that reference – inside or outside the text? Pay particular attention to the use of *I* and *we* in this poem.
▷ Where do references change from being situation reference to text reference?

she being Brand

-new;and you
know consequently a
5 *little stiff i was*
careful of her and(having

thoroughly oiled the universal
joint tested my gas felt of
10 *her radiator made sure her springs were O.*

K.)i went right to it flooded-the-carburetor cranked her

up,slipped the
15 *clutch(and then somehow got into reverse she*
kicked what
the hell)next
minute i was back in neutral tried and

20 *again slo-wly;bare,ly nudg. ing(my*

lev-er Right-
oh and her gears being in
A 1 shape passed
25 *from low through*
second-in-to-high like
greased lightning)just as we turned the corner of Divinity

avenue i touched the accelerator and give
30
her the juice,good

(it

35 *was the first ride and believe i we was*
happy to see how nice she acted right up to
the last minute coming back down by the Public
Gardens i slammed on

the
40 *internalexpanding*
&
externalcontracting
brakes Bothatonce and

45 *brought allof her tremB*
-ling
to a:dead.

stand-
50 *;Still)*

[e. e. cummings *Selected Poems 1923–1958*, Faber, 1960]

There are two 'main' pronouns in the poem, *i* and *she/her*. If we ask who is *i* here, and who is *she/her*, we cannot easily find the answers to those questions in the text itself. We could say that *she* is the car that is being driven in the poem, but it is obvious that this is not the whole story. To find the answers, we have to look outside the passage and into the context, or situation, of the poem.

We could say that the *i* (or, more usually, capital *I*) is the 'writer' of the poem. We could also say that the *I* is the driver of the car, who is 'telling us' the poem; so that it is not the writer who is the *I*, but a narrator created by the writer to speak the poem for him. In cumming's poem, the *I* is a character in the poem – *I* is the driver of the car. The poem is written using what is called first-person narrative.

We could say that the *she/her* figure in the poem is the car, or that it is a woman. Because we are uncertain of whose point of view is being given, this ambiguity creates what, today, we would see as the highly sexist nature of the poem.

ACTIVITY 4

Look back at the extract on p. 12. How does the writer play with the idea of text and situation reference in this passage?

The way in which writers play with text and situation reference is very important. It has important effects and implications that you should try to understand at this point. Look back at the extracts in this chapter so far.

▷ What is the major difference between the use of reference on the magazine cover and the use of reference in the other texts that you have read so far?

The important difference is that the reference words on the magazine cover don't actually refer to other words around them; they don't refer to the nearest text – because there isn't any. They refer to things inside the magazine. To call them cataphoric in the strict sense is cheating. But the reference words do refer forward, even if the reference seems to be on the borderline of text and situation reference.

▷ Why do magazine editors use reference words in this way on the covers of magazine?

WRITING ACTIVITY B

1 Look at paragraphs **1** and **2** on page 11. Using these texts as a model, write the introductory paragraph to an article about, or a profile of, a person you know or admire. Before you start to write, make sure that you establish who your audience is: a major problem with the text about the cat on page 9 is that the child writing the piece has little idea of the audience who will read it.

2 Look at the e. e. cummings poem again. Rewrite part or all of the text from the point of view of the woman/car. Before you do so, think about what information you would need from the poem to rewrite it. Take some notes, particularly from the first 10–15 lines. Think about the way in which you would need to reverse the perspective from the driver to the driven.

2.1.3 **Demonstratives**

Demonstratives consist of a particular group of words:

1	2
this	*that*
these	*those*
here	*there*
now	*then*

▷ What is the main difference between the words in column 1 and the words in column 2?

Think about this very carefully, because it is fundamental to the effects that these words have, and the functions that they perform, in our language. The basic job of these words can be seen in the following:

> *Do you want these ones?*
> *No, I want those ones?*

They help us to point to things – and the pointing function can happen more often in speech than in writing. In terms of written language, we can often find this group of words in written conversation, such as in the example that we have just read. But these words do occur in written texts. You have just read the phrase *these words* twice in the space of seven lines, excluding the dialogue. What does *these words* refer to here?

You can see that this group of words is often used with nouns – for example, *these words* and *this group*.

ACTIVITY 5

Now look at the following two extracts. As you read them, decide what purpose the texts have. Find the demonstratives in them. Are the demonstratives from column 1 or column 2? Do these demonstratives point into or away from the things that they are linked to, and what effect does that pointing have?

> *LINK machines will give you two balance figures. One of these is the account balance and shows you how much money was in your account at the end of the previous working day. The second figure is the available balance; this shows the maximum amount of cash you can actually withdraw.*

[NatWest leaflet PO 006, April 1997]

> *[Mabel Strickland] wielded considerable influence, both through her journalism and her formidable personality, but her political career cannot be accounted a success. She attributed this to her sex rather than her policies, and would often clutch at her ample breasts and moan: 'If it wasn't for these I would be Prime Minister of Malta!'*

[H. Massingberd (ed.), *The Daily Telegraph Book of Obituaries*, 1994]

Demonstratives are essentially words that point. You have just seen here that the column 1 words *this* and *these* create immediacy and intimacy because they point towards things that are immediately important to the speaker or writer. These are the effects that they have.

ACTIVITY 6

Now read the following extract from *A White Merc with Fins*, by James Hawes. In this extract the main figure in the book, who is a university graduate and who 'tells the story', has just gone into a pub to pick the pockets of some lads he has found there. As you read the passage decide what kind of person the speaker is:

> *I looked at <u>this</u> gang of lads who had been to Colleges and were now having a good time with their suits off, and I had a serious bout of the horrors that said: How the hell did I end up like <u>this</u>, nicking wallets in pubs? How did the dream, the middle-class dream of sugar and sunshine, come to an end?*
>
> *Really, they should not send people like us to Colleges. It is bullshit, they might as well be honest and make us go to work in banks when we are eighteen, or else only let us into Colleges to do teaching certs or accountancy or stuff like <u>that</u>. Instead, you get three years of the interesting stuff and then they tell you: OK lads and lassies, the good news is: you now have the legal right to wear a fucking stupid hat and gown (to prove you are intelligent).*
>
> *The bad news is: <u>that</u>'s it.*
>
> [James Hawes, *A White Merc with Fins*, Vintage, 1996]

1 What do the two words 'this' and the two 'that's, which have been underlined for you, refer to? Do they refer to one word, to a group of words or to an idea contained in the passage?

2 What is the speaker's attitude to the things that *this* and *that* refer to?

3 Is the speaker close to those things or distant from them?

4 Which word – *this* or *that* – refers to the things that he is close to and those that he is distant from?

You have just seen that *this* and *that* can refer to one word, to a group of words or to an idea. Now read through the following text and decide whether *this* and *that* refer to things or to ideas:

> *Man at airport: I'd like this bag to go to Moscow. This one to New York, and this one to Helsinki.*
>
> *Steward: I'm sorry sir. We can't do that.*
>
> *Man at airport: Nonsense. That's what you did last time I flew with you.*
>
> [*The Bumper Book of 3001 Jokes*, Cliveden Press, 1989]

There is one other thing to be said about *this*, *that*, *these* and *those*. You have seen that these words can either occur by themselves – as in *this shows the maximum amount* – or with a noun, as in *these words*. However, we hardly ever use *this* or *that* by themselves to refer to humans, but only for things or objects.

Imagine this scene at the dentist's. A box of dental equipment has arrived in the dentist's front office. The dentist arrives and says to the receptionist:

> *OK, Sue, I'll take that through.*

Imagine that a patient arrives. What would be his or her reaction if the dentist were to use the same words?

There are exceptions to this situation, in sentences such as the following:

That is the man who used to be a Conservative MP.
And this must be your delightful baby boy.

As you can see, 'this' or 'that' refers to humans, usually when someone is being identified.

ACTIVITY 7

Look through all the examples of *this*, *that*, *these* and *those* that you have looked at in this section. Change all the *this*'s for the *that*'s, and vice versa; and change the *these*'s for all the *those*'s. What is the effect in each case?

2.1.4 'Here', 'there', 'now' and 'then'

Look at this example from the NatWest leaflet that you studied before:

Most NatWest cash machines now give you details of payments going into or out of your account first thing in the morning. These are called provisional morning entries.

Imagine someone looking back on that development in five years' time.

▷ What would that person write?
▷ What would the words *now*, in the passage above, and *then*, in the passage you created, refer to in each case?
▷ Would you also have to change the word *these*?
▷ If you did, why would you have to change it?

Look at this next text and decide what the word *there* refers to:

[Sir Melford Stevenson] once told a man acquitted of rape: 'I see you come from Slough. It is a terrible place. You can go back there.'

[H. Massingberd (ed.), *The Daily Telegraph Book of Obituaries*, 1994]

The words *here*, *there*, *now* and *then* are known as **demonstrative adverbs**.

WRITING ACTIVITY C

Find examples of the kinds of leaflets that you have just looked at; leaflets that describe a service that is going to be provided. Look at how the demonstratives that you have just read about are used.

Imagine that your local swimming baths is going to have a special 'Women only' hour on a Tuesday evening. The local council is going to provide a mobile crèche. Write a leaflet that the swimming baths can hand out to advertise the service.

Alternatively, write your own leaflet about a service that is going to be provided and that interests you personally.

1 What does the use of demonstratives in leaflets tell you about the place and use of demonstratives in general?

2 Are the effects of intimacy and distance as important in writing leaflets as they are in writing prose fiction?

2.1.5 Comparatives

In the following sentences, A is compared to B:

1 *That duck was less tasty than the last one you cooked us* – in which *that duck* is compared to *the last one you cooked us.*

2 *I think that Spungo is a much better washing powder than WashRite* – in which *Spungo* is compared to *WashRite.*

3 *All my life I've been waiting for a Labour government that is as compassionate as a Conservative one* – in which *a Labour government* is compared to *a Conservative one.*

You can see that the comparisons link or draw together the things being compared. But there are complications in this area. The first complication is that comparisons **1**, **2** and **3** occur within the sentence and so don't directly contribute to cohesion. The second point to be made is that comparison occurs in two main ways:

- Where things are the same, as in **3** above.
- Where things are similar.

However, sometimes comparisons aren't as explicit or clear as those three examples.

Read the following, which comes from a series of interviews with people who have moved out of London into the countryside:

> *I've also lost out a little on commuting: if I'm working in Edinburgh or Glasgow it takes me an hour to drive in, whereas in London it took me half an hour – but to travel five miles… we are less likely to be burgled but the possible consequences are more serious as we are a long way from help. However there is much more sense of belonging and community – little things like the butcher knowing where to deliver because he remembers scrumping apples from the orchard.*

[*The Guardian*, 7 August 1994]

▷ What do the phrases *a little, less likely, more serious* and *much more sense* refer to, and what comparison is being made?
▷ Is that reference to quantity, to a comparison in terms of number or to quality here?
▷ How do those comparisons help the message of the paragraph?

ACTIVITY 8

1 Compare the comparative expressions that you have just looked at with the following:

> *A picture of a more insecure Britain – with greater change in both jobs and family life – emerged yesterday from a series of interviews with 9,000 people in 5,000 households. … Professor Gershuny, director of the project said: 'More and more firms are demanding a flexible workforce, which means temporary contracts, laying off and taking up employment again as new markets open. Under these conditions it is likely women will fill such openings. … Many men in full time core jobs will build up important skills and specialisms that are very marketable. In an economy becoming more dependent on specialised skills, movement to self-employment as high status, highly paid consultants will increasingly provide rich pickings for such men.*

[*The Guardian*, 6 September 1994]

In this passage, there is an example of a comparison of quality and two examples of comparisons in terms of quantity. Can you identify them?

2 In addition, there are two other examples of particular types of comparison. Look at the following expressions as they are organised here:

> *'such openings' as …?*
> *'such men' as …?*

How does the word *such* in this situation create similarity? Again, are we talking in terms of quantity or quality here?

WRITING ACTIVITY D

1 Articles such as the one above that report the 'state of Britain' or attitudes in Britain are commonly published in newspapers such as *The Guardian* and *The Times*. In addition, there are books such as *Whitaker's Almanac* and *Britain 1996*, which will provide you with tables of information about Britain. Look at one of those tables and write a piece that compares and contrasts aspects of life in Britain today. In addition, check Section 2.4 of this chapter, which examines the way in which we use connectives to show contrast.

2 Survey some of your friends or class colleagues about attitudes to the school or college restaurant food. Make sure that the questions are carefully written so that you only get 'yes/no' answers. Look at the results in terms of things such as the sex, age and domestic status (that is, living alone, with parents, with a partner, and so on) of the respondents. Write up your results in a short passage. Look carefully at how you use comparatives. Where do you use comparisons of quality (*worst/better*, easiest to use, and so on) and where do you use comparisons of quantity (*more/fewer* and so on)?

2.2 Substitution

Look at the following, which is from an article describing the launch of a new radio station, XFM, in London:

> *Its format – 'cutting edge' alternative rock and indie music – may confine it to a relative small niche. However, it is a clearly defined one, which attracts a youthful and probably loyal audience, and one which is potentially attractive to advertisers.*

> [*Ariel* (BBC in-house magazine), 28 January 1997]

▷ What do the two *one*'s stand for from the rest of the passage?

We can see that they stand for – or **substitute** for – the word *niche*, which occurs earlier in the passage. We can take the word *one* out of each position and put the words *niche* or *a niche* in its place.

Now look at this:

> *She married ma Grandad first likes, a chacin auld cowboy fae County Wexford. The auld dude used tae sit ma Ma oan his lap n sing tae hur: Irish rebel songs, likesay. He hud hair growin oot ay his nostrils n she though thit he wis ancient, the wey ankle-biters do, likes.*

> [Irving Welsh, *Trainspotting*, Minerva, 1992]

▷ What does the word *do* stand for?

Now imagine a sixth-form student in a hurry to get to the pub, saying to a lecturer:

> *Student: 'Can I leave my laptop in your office overnight, Mr Clegg?'*
> *Sarcastic lecturer: 'I think not'.*

▷ What is *not* a substitute for here?

A very limited group of words is used for substitution:

> *one, ones, the same*
> *do*
> *so, not*

2.2.1 'One', 'ones' and 'the same'

'One' and 'ones'

This group of words replaces nouns. If we go back to the extract about the indie radio station, we can see that *one* replaces the noun *niche*.

Look at these examples and decide which nouns the words *one* or *ones* are substituting for in each case:

1   *I do wish Sue would settle down. These men ... she has a different one each week.*

2   *A: Which of these tops should I choose?*
    B: How about the green one?
    A: Well, yes, if I wanted to wear something on the slab.

3   *A: Have you finished your psychology essay?*
    B: Yes, but now I've got an English lit. one which I have to give in on Thursday.

In each case, we can see which noun from the previous sentence is substituted in the second:

> one – *man*   one – *top*   one – *essay*.

The important effect of substitution here is that it reinforces a contrast. In **1**, the words *a different* contrast each man that Sue has with the other men. In **2**, the words *the green* contrast that particular top with any of the others in the shop. And in **3**, the words *an English lit.* contrast that essay with the psychology essay. The contrasts are also important because they highlight the way in which this particular kind of substitution is built. In each case the word *one* is modified by other words – *a different one; the green one; an English lit one which I have to give in on Thursday.*

Where *one* is used for substitution it is always modified, either before or after the noun: this is an important test for *one* used in substitution.

Another test for *one* as substitute is to put the noun that is being substituted into the plural. Where *one* is a substitute, the plural is always *ones* rather than *some*.

Now look at this extract from an interview with the actor, Paul Nicholls, from an issue of a teenage magazine:

> *I haven't got a particular 'type', but the one thing I do hate is stuck up girls who think they're just the best thing in the world! The most attractive girls are the ones who*

don't realise how beautiful they are! I just want a girl who'll be there for me…
someone to give me a good hug when I need one.

[*Sugar*, no. 24, October 1996]

Now read the passage out loud to yourself.

If you stress the word *one*, then it is always *one* as a number, as in: *One of the things I hate about him is his choice of clothes* or *There was only one piece of cake left.*

If it is unstressed, it is either *one* as substitution, or *one* as ellipsis. Look back over what you have just read and decide how you can tell between the two.

We can now summarise the use of *one* as a substitute:

1 It is only used for countable nouns. Why can't you say:

> *A: I'd like rice please.*
> *B: Would you like the yellow one?*

and how would you have to rewrite the reply so that it makes sense?

2 *One* is always modified:

> *A: Would you like the red carnation?*
> *B: No, I'd like the pink one with the short stem, please.*

3 *One* is never used for names:

> *A: Have you seen John?*
> *B: Well, I saw the tall one a minute ago.*

4 *One* is never used for compound nouns:

> *A: Have you seen the new soap opera?*
> *B: No, but I've seen the new classical one.*

5 *One* is stressed in speech when it is a numeral:

> *It was just one of those things.*

6 *One* is unstressed in speech when it is the substitute or the ellipsis:

> *Your social life will be fantastic this month – you've got so many party invites, you don't know which one to accept first.*

Use test **2** to decide if this is substitution or ellipsis, but just be careful with the second example.

You can now tell the difference between *one* as a number, *one* as substitution and *one* as ellipsis. But where does it all get you?

WRITING ACTIVITY E

1 There are many contrasts of the kind that we have looked at in the advice sections and agony columns of newspapers and magazines. Why do you think this is so? Look at some agony columns. Now invent your own problems, write a letter to the doctor, or the agony aunt/uncle and then set out their reply. Note the number of times that you use *one* in its various forms in the pieces that you write. Note the other kinds of contrastive forms.

2 Write a 'spoof' interview with a current actor or actress. Make sure that this person gives lots of opinions of their own. Again, note how many times you use the word *one* in its various forms in the interview.

'The same'

The expression *the same* is usually found in the following settings:

- With *but* and / or *with/without* – for example:

     A: *Jim wants a bacon butty and chips.*
     B: *I'll have the same, but without the chips.*

- With *say/thought/realise* and so on, where *the same* applies to a fact or idea – for example:

     A: *I don't think you can build that house there.*
     B: *No, and Phil thinks the same.*

- In the sense of *do the same* – for example:

     And as for faithfulness, if a girlfriend two-timed me, I suppose I'd think it'd be OK to do the same.

     [*Sugar*, no. 24, October 1996]

- As *be the same*, sometimes with an adverb such as *quite*, *nearly* or *almost* – for example:

     One thing we do miss is the range of shopping. Exeter is OK but it's not quite the same.

     [*The Guardian*, 7 August 1994]

You can see, I hope, that in each case *the same* substitutes for some earlier item.

▷ Go through each of the four examples given here. In each case, what does *the same* substitute for?

2.2.2 'Do'

Look at the following text. As you are doing so, answer the following questions:

▷ What words does *do* substitute for here?
▷ What parts of speech are the words that have been substituted?

   *When I first met Jo I thought she was brilliant. I still do – it's just that she's a bit …
   clingy, I suppose.*

     [*Bliss*, August 1996]

This second question is important – make sure you get it right.

You can see from this example that the substitute *do* works through all its forms: *do, does, did, doing, done*. You can also see from this example that *do* can substitute and change tense at the same time; in this case from the past-tense *met* to the present-tense *do*. Changing tense can often be important. This is because, like *one* in the previous section, the effect of substitution with *do* is often to suggest a contrast.

▷ What contrast is going on between the first sentence and the second sentence in the above example?

ACTIVITY 9

Now look through these pairs of statements. Decide what substitutions are being made and also what the contrasts are:

1 *Bill gave up smoking ten years ago. His wife did the following year.*

2 *A: I should have wormed the cat before now.*
 B: Well, somebody should do soon.

3 *It's time to admit you've made a mistake. If you don't do, you'll only dig yourself into an even bigger hole. (Be careful with this example.)*

4 *A: I finally sorted it all out.*
 B: It was high time you did.

As with a number of the examples that we looked at in the section about *one*, where *do* is used for a substitute it is not usually stressed in speech.

In addition, *do* is often used after other auxiliary verbs, such as *may, will, might, have, used to*. Again, the effect is to emphasise a contrast:

A: Has he wormed the cat?
B: He might have done.
A: None of those English Language students passed.
B: No, but they could have done, if they'd worked harder.
A: Does she smoke now?
B: No, but she used to do when she was younger.

ACTIVITY 10

Look at the following passage of speech, taken from a conversation between teachers in a school for students learning English as a Foreign Language. As you look at the extract, decide what you think that the teachers are talking about:

H: I think that people actually hang on to their pronunciation. There's an identity thing.
E: Mm.
P: Ooh yeah. I mean there might be…
H: National and individual.
E: Yeah that's it.
J: Course they do.

[courtesy of Keith Richards]

1 What does *do* substitute for in J's turn at the end of the extract?

2 Read the extract out loud with some others. Is the *do* stressed, or not?

3 Is there a contrast going on between the *do* and the substituted item? What does this tell you about the idea that substitution is usually used for contrast?

4 Why do you think that J is able to substitute *do* when three other people have spoken, one of them twice, between her *do* and the verb for which it substitutes?

5 What do you think this extract tells you about the use of *do* as a substitute in conversation?

6 How effective is it as a 'binding agent' in conversation?

It is possible for *do* to be coupled with *so*, in the phrase *do so*. Unfortunately, and just to complicate matters, *do so* is only possible where substitute *do* is used to indicate a contrast.

ACTIVITY 11

Go back through all the examples that you've read in this section on *do*. Replace each *do* with *do so*.

1 Which of these replacements seems to work, and which doesn't?

2 As you are doing this, read the replacements out to yourself. Is the *do* in these places stressed or unstressed?

3 If *do so* is not possible, what do you think that means? Look back through the examples in this section.

It is also usual to use *do so* in questions and commands. For example:

> A: *I haven't fed the cat.*
> B: *Will you do so at once, please?*

> A: *I haven't fed the cat.*
> B: *Please do so at once!*

▷ What kind of tone does using *do so* suggest here?
▷ What kind of people might use *do so* in these kinds of circumstances?
▷ Is there any kind of contrast going on here?

Do is used for a number of other purposes; often, where it is used in combination with other words. In these combinations, *do* is not being used as a verb substitute.

We use *do, does, doesn't, don't, did, didn't* as **auxiliary verbs**:

● In questions: *It sounds like the two of you get on well, so why don't you ask him out?*
● In negatives: *I know my parents are worried about me, but I don't know how to make them understand how I feel.*
● In 'tag-questions': *You really think this song is about you, don't you?*
● When something is being emphasised: *I was certain he really did love me.*

Do can also mean to perform an action. Notice that in situations like this, *do* is often followed by *it* or *this/that*:

> *I'm obsessed with cleaning my teeth. I do it about five times a day.*

> [*Bliss*, June 1996]

> *Be wonderfully kind, caring and attentive to him. Do this for long enough to make sure he knows he's onto a good thing – you.*

> [*Bliss*, June 1996]

Note here that you can replace *do it/this/that* with *do so*. Again, the effect is very formal.

Do is also used in specific **collocations** in phrases such as *doing the dishes*, *do the dirty on somebody* and *do 100 mph*.

2.2.3 'So' and 'not'

'So'

You have just seen that *one* and *ones* substitute for nouns, and that *do* substitutes for verbs. In this section we will look at how *so* and *not* substitute for larger stretches of language: they substitute for clauses, usually *that* clauses. It is convenient here for 'clause' to mean a group of words that includes a subject and a finite verb. If you are unsure of these terms, please look them up. However, here's an example:

> A: Did Mary bring the disc back?
> B: I think so.

What does *so* substitute for here? We could rewrite the reply here as:

> B: I think that Mary brought the disc back.

where the words *that Mary brought the disc back* replace or substitute for the word *so* in the original answer. The clause *that Mary brought the disc back* contains a subject, *Mary*, and a verb, *brought*. It also contains an object, *the disc*, and an adverb, *back*. Objects and complements won't always be necessary, as in:

> A: Did Mary understand?
> B: I think so.

▷ What does *so* substitute for here?

One of the happy things about *so* as a substitute is that it tends to occur in a number of very specific environments. It is these environments that help us to see the purposes for, and effects of, using *so* as a substitute:

● *So* tends to follow 'reporting' verbs, such as *tell* and *say* – for example:
> A: Paul is a complete fool with a bit of drink in him.
> B: I should say so.

> A: I don't think Peter should buy that car
> B: Well tell him so.

● We use *so* in these circumstances when we are talking about the authority for a statement. Compare these two examples:
> 1   A: That teacher's no good.
>   B: Who says so?
>   A: I say so.

> 2   A: That teacher's no good.
>   B: Who says that?
>   A: I do.

In **1**, speaker – wants to know why he or she should believe the statement. In **2**, speaker – just wants to know who has said the words; so he or she uses *that*. The effect of *so* in this kind of situation is to establish authority: in **1**, speaker A feels he or she has the authority to denounce the teacher.

● We also use *so* with so-called 'verbs of cognition': *believe, hope, expect, imagine, suppose, guess, reckon, think, be afraid*. Here again, *so* substitutes for a *that* clause:

A: Is that your parents?
B: I'm afraid so. (= I'm afraid that it is my parents.)

A: Do you think City will get stuffed on Saturday?
B: I hope so. (= I hope that City will get stuffed on Saturday.)

● *So* can also be used at the beginning of a clause with verbs such as *say*, *hear*, *understand*, *tell* and *believe*. As you read these examples, consider what the attitude of speaker – is to what speaker A says:

A: Peter's got a place at UMIST.
B: So I heard.

A: The Canaries must go down this season.
B: So you keep saying.

A: Everybody in the world has a double.
B: So they say.

ACTIVITY 12
Can you tell anything about the 'class' of the people in the following extracts?

'Do you go to much of this sort of thing?' he asked when they were driving home.
'Oh, now and then,' said Lucy, who had rather enjoyed herself.
'Is it typical of county society?'
'I suppose so. Mother, would it be?'
'Plenty of society,' said Mrs Honeychurch, who was trying to remember the hang of one of the dresses.

[E. M. Forster, *A Room with a View*, Penguin, 1990]

MAID: It's the dress, madam, that every lady wears in the country, but when she visits or receives company.
MISS HARDCASTLE: And are you sure he does not remember my face or person?
MAID: Certain of it.
MISS HARDCASTLE: I vow I thought so; for though we spoke for some time together, yet his fears were such, that he never once looked up during the interview.

[Oliver Goldsmith, *She Stoops to Conquer*, Act III, Scene I, ll. 231–238]

Does the class of people in these extracts tell you anything about the use of *so*?

'Not'
Not is used instead of *so* when the substitute clause is negative, but this use seems even more formal than the use of *so*:

Besides, the wench was not uncomely.
'The third test?' she said.
'Am I to be weaponless again?' said Hrun.
Liessa reached up and removed her helmet, letting the coils of red hair tumble out.
Then she unfastened the brooch of her robe. Underneath, she was naked. ...
As she raised a hand and proffered a glass of wine she smiled, and said, 'I think not.'

[Terry Pratchett, *The Colour of Magic*, Corgi, 1983]

The phrase *I think not* can also be very sarcastic.

In fact, the use of *not* as a substitute for *think, expect* and *believe* is very rare – and it is partly the rarity value that makes it so formal. *Not* as a substitute is not used with *tell* and only occasionally with *say*, where *say* is always preceded by a **modal auxiliary verb**, such as *may, might* or *should*:

> A: *Could you lend me a fiver till the Coop pays me?*
> B: *I should say not after last night's little episode!*

There is one further use of *so* as a substitute that we have to consider here. That is where *so* is used at the beginning of a clause:

> A: *That band they've got on at the Met. had great reviews for its last album.*
> B: *So I hear.*

> A: *If you stand at Eros' statue in Piccadilly for the rest of your life, you'll eventually meet everybody you know.*
> B: *So they say.*

▷ Does speaker – quite believe A in each of these cases?
▷ What, then, is the effect of putting *so* at the beginning of the clauses in each case?

Other non-cohesive uses of 'so'

There are a number of other ways in which we use the word *so*. Here we will mention just two:

> *So' used to mean 'therefore'; ie., 'He speaks very little English, so I talked to him through an interpreter'*
> *'So' is also used as an 'intensifier', emphasise things; ie., 'I'm so glad you could come. I've never felt so lonely in my life.'*

> [*Cobuild English Language Dictionary*, Collins, 1987]

ACTIVITY 13

Look through all the examples of *not* and *so* that you have looked at in this section. Read them out loud to yourself.

1 What kind of tone of voice has to be used in each case?

2 What does that tell you about the effects of *so* and *not*, and why they are used in each case?

2.3 Ellipsis

In a great many places in both writing and speech, we leave words out when we know, or think, that the reader or listener will know what we mean and will fill in the words themselves. Look at the following three examples. In each case, the place where a word or phrase is missing is indicated with the symbol '>'. Try to work out what word could be placed in the spaces:

1 *The characters are likeable, > flawed and opinionated, and > much sassier than their seventies counterparts.*

> [*Radio Times*, 28 June – 4 July 1997]

2   *A variety of acoustic basses were brought in, and I did what every musician should –
instead of looking at the brand name, I used the same judge that the audience uses –
> ears.*

[Bassist, March 1997]

3   *'Sorry' said Mrs Crumb, putting her hand to her ear 'Can you speak up please!'
'I'D . . . LIKE . . . A . . . LOAF . . . OF . . . BREAD!!!' roared Mr Noisy.
'> Can't hear you' replied Mrs Crumb.
Mr Noisy gave up and went out.*

[Roger Hargreaves, Mr Noisy, Thurman Publishing, 1976]

These passages could be rewritten as follows:

1a   *The characters are likeable, (the characters are) flawed and opinionated, and (the
characters are) much sassier than their seventies counterparts.*

2a   *A variety of acoustic basses were brought in, and I did what every musician should –
instead of looking at the brand name, I used the same judge that the audience uses – (I
used [my])ears.*

3a   *'Sorry' said Mrs Crumb, putting her hand to her ear 'Can your speak up please!'
'I'D . . . LIKE . . . A . . . LOAF . . . OF . . . BREAD!!!' roared Mr Noisy.
'(I)Can't hear you' replied Mrs Crumb.
Mr Noisy gave up and went out.*

We could rewrite in this way – but we don't need to, because we 'understand'
the things that are missed out. In fact, if we included them every time we wrote,
our writing style would be laborious and boring. This is even more true of spoken
language.

We can divide <u>ellipsis</u> into three types: **noun ellipsis**; **verb ellipsis** and **clause
ellipsis**.

2.3.1 Noun ellipsis

At this point, it is useful to try to understand the way in which we order words
before a noun.

▷ What is wrong with the following phrase?

   Bantam those golden four brown eggs.

The problem is that we instinctively feel that the words in front of *eggs* are in the
wrong order. The linguistic computers that are our brains want to 'auto-sort' them
into the right order:

   Those four golden brown bantam eggs.

This is because the words that we put in front of nouns fall into certain
categories, and the categories themselves follow a certain pattern before the
nouns at the head of the phrase:

Deictic	Numbers	Adjectives	Nouns
Those	*four*	*golden brown*	*bantam*

<u>Deictics</u> include possessives such as *mine, yours, his, hers, its, ours, theirs*, or
so-called 'genitives', such as *Fred's* or *the cat's*; **demonstratives** such as *this, that,
those, these*; and a group of words that includes items such as *each, all, both, any,
either, none, neither, some.*

Numbers include not only the **cardinal** numbers (*one, two, three* and so on) but also the **ordinals** (*first, second, third, fourth* and so on), and also some 'general numbers', such as *next, last, other*.

Adjectives include all of the obvious adjectives, but ellipsis can often follow **comparative** and **superlative** adjectives; that is, the *-er* and *-est* forms. In addition, adjectives that express size, age, shape, colour and origin – usually in that order – can also occur in elliptical expressions.

Nouns used before the head noun in the noun phrase are used to classify the head noun. These may occur in compound noun combinations such as *car park, kitchen cupboard, railway station* and *milk bottle*. Alternatively – and more useful here – are compound nouns where the first noun of the compound is a material or substance, such as *leather apron* or *plastic raincoat*, or where the noun indicates a use or purpose, such as *winter dress* or *garden chair*.

ACTIVITY 14

1 As before, contrast, operates very strongly here, as these examples will show. The ellipsis is again indicated with a '>'; work out what words should go into the spaces:

This was not the first time that two pickups appeared on the Star bass. As stated earlier, Jet's > had two, but his > had four rotary control knobs (two for Volume and two for Tone) whereas this > features a single volume and two rotary switches.

[*Bassist*, March 1997]

Civil servants in the Whitehall jungle have much the same stress problems as baboons on the Serengeti plains, a Canadian health researcher pointed out yesterday. Both > live in hierarchical structures. Both > are bothered about status.

[*The Guardian*, 6 September 1994]

Scandinavia tops the western world with nigh on every woman breast-feeding to start off with and three out of four > still going strong at three months. England and Wales manage six out of ten > at birth, dropping to a disappointing one in four > by four months. Scotland and Ireland fare even worse.

[*Radio Times*, 28 June – 4 July 1997]

On board our ships – two of the largest > and most luxurious > on the Irish Sea – facilities are second to none.

[Irish Ferries advertisement]

My earliest memories of wallflowers flood back at seed-sowing time: my grandfather grew them … And the varieties he grew are still available today – the dusky crimson 'Blood Red' >, fiery orange 'Vulcan' >, and the brilliant yellow 'Cloth of Gold' >.

[adapted from *Radio Times*, 14–20 June 1997]

He wanted to buy his wife the cotton top. Instead she chose the silk >.

2 Look through texts, particularly from magazines and newspapers, and pick out examples of noun ellipsis. Why is noun ellipsis something that you can often find in 'disposable' media such as newspapers and magazines? Why can you can find fewer examples in 'lasting' media such as books? What do the answers to those questions tell you about the effects of noun ellipsis?

2.3.2 Verb ellipsis

Verb ellipsis happens in two particular ways. The first is when the main verb and elements to the right of the verb in the main phrase are lost. Look at these examples, and as you do so think about the contrast that is being made.

> *I thought I had picked up all the equipment I needed. Unfortunately I hadn't >.*

> *Peter never did learn to type with more than one finger. In all those years he probably should have >.*

Verbal ellipsis of this kind can perform a number of functions:

- It can make a contrast between the subjects of actions, the subjects of the verbs:

  > *My brother came running in one day. He said, 'Mum, mum, I've got a monster up my nose.'*
  > *My mum said, 'You haven't.'*
  > *He said, 'I have. It's a bogeyman.'*
  >
  > [*The Bumper Book of 3001 Jokes*, Cliveden Press, 1989]

- It can make a contrast between obligations or possibilities:

  > *David wanted her to stay the night. Alice told him that she couldn't.*

- Sometimes the contrast is made using the verb *be*:

  > *He thought it was hereditary in his case. Well it might be.*
  >
  > [*Cobuild English Grammar*, HarperCollins, 1990]

Note that in the first two cases above the contrast is emphasised by the use of negatives. Negatives very often perform this elliptical function.

Another area in which this kind of ellipsis operates is in responses that show surprise:

> *A: David works for them now.*
> *B: Does he?*

> *A: There's someone in the garden.*
> *B: Is there?*

> *A: I can never believe a word that woman says.*
> *B: Can't you?*

The second kind of verb ellipsis is where the subject and other elements to the left of the main verb are left out. This too is particularly present in conversation:

> *A: What's Peter doing?*
> *B: > Minding his own business.*

> *There's that strange man again. > Driving around in his damned big car, > winding the windows down and > taking photos.*

Both types of verb ellipsis can be present when replies are very colloquial and informal, such as this from a four-year-old:

> *A: Have Liam and Sammy gone on holiday?*
> *B: Might have.*

ACTIVITY 15

Look at the following texts. Where is the ellipsis and which type of ellipsis is happening here: to the right or left of the main verb?

'It's the tree,' said the dryad shortly.
'What's it doing?' said Rincewind.
'Living.'

[Terry Pratchett, *The Colour of Magic*, Corgi, 1983]

'One cannot hurry these things,' said the old alchemist peevishly. 'Assaying takes time. Ah.' He prodded the saucer, where the coin now lay in a swirl of green colour. He made some calculations on a scrap of parchment.
   'Exceptionally interesting,' he said at last.

[Terry Pratchett, *The Colour of Magic*, Corgi, 1983]

... your skull still croons
Lascivious catches and indecent tunes;
And croaks; Ashes to ashes, dust to dust.
Pray God be with you in your lust.
And God immediately is, but such a one
Whose skin stinks like a herring in the sun,...

[from 'The Nuptial Torches', Tony Harrison, *Selected Poems*, Penguin, 1987]

His features yield no clues to why he has become what he has. But neither does his background.

[*The Daily Telegraph*, 3 April 1997]

Q. What do you think of the criticism that you are not very good?
George. We're not.

[Geoffrey Guiliano, *The Beatles: a Celebration*, Select Editions, 1985]

2.3.3 Clause ellipsis

Clause ellipsis is often more difficult to pin down. Some of that difficulty occurs because **linguists** and **grammarians** often have differing ideas as to what a **clause** is. For the sake of simplicity, I shall define a clause as a group of words that contains a subject and a **finite verb**. For example, from the last sentence we could make three sentences, and therefore three clauses:

I shall define a clause.
A clause is a group of words.
A clause contains a subject and a finite verb.

There are three grammatical subjects: *I*, *A clause* and *A clause* again. There are also three finite verb phrases: *shall define*, *is* and *contains*.

The original combined sentence contains two complete clauses: *I shall define a clause...* and *that contains a subject and a finite verb*.

One of the main areas of clause ellipsis is in replies to questions, where the person who is replying avoid repeating words used in the question:

A: Where did you grow up then?
B: Cardiff.

A: How are you feeling?
B: Awful.

A: Where did the money come from?
B: Me dad.

When you want to emphasise your own feelings, replies can also be formed from adverbs and adverbial phrases:

A: Is this entirely between us?
B: Absolutely.

A: Has she been ill?
B: Not really.

ACTIVITY 16

1   In the speech of teenagers and young people, the words used in reply can be part of linguistic fashion. At the time of writing, the phrase *no way* is current:

> *A: Echobelly have fired their singer.*
> *B: No way!*

In this situation, ellipsis becomes subject to social factors. Why do you think this could be? Why do you think that ellipsis emphasises the feelings? Can you think of other short replies that emphasise feelings?

2   Ellipsis can also be used in replies when you wish to show agreement, by using the words *too, so, neither, either*. What words are being left out in the replies to the following statements? What are the differences in the use of *too, neither* and *either*. What differences in formality are there between the pairs of statements and replies?

> *A: I couldn't understand a word of that.*
> *B: I couldn't either.*
>
> *A: I'm knackered.*
> *B: I am too.*
>
> *A: God, I'm in love with that woman.*
> *B: Yes, I am too.*
>
> *A: I couldn't find the money.*
> *B: Neither could Peter.*
>
> *A: I'm being serious here.*
> *B: So am I.*
>
> *A: I'm not joking, you know.*
> *B: Neither am I.*
>
> *A: I told Mike what was happening to the book.*
> *B: Ah, so did I.*

Another kind of ellipsis occurs when what is left of the clause is a 'wh' question word: *when, where, which, who, whose, how.* For example:

> *I put that book down here somewhere. But God knows where.*
> *We have to deal with the damp in the basement and the plague of mice and cockroaches. The question is how?*

ACTIVITY 17

1 Look at the following passage from a TV magazine. As you read the extract, decide what kind of audience it is written for. What kind of tone is used here: How formal is it? How near is it to the conversational tone you have just read in the above examples? What examples of ellipsis can you find? Think about your answers in the above examples. Why do you think ellipsis is used here?

> *DRAMA*
> *Friends*
> *9.00pm C4*
>
> *Pour yourself another espresso, turn off the mobile phone and settle back in the company of your favourite* Friends. *The American Sitcom is back for a third series and it's a corker.*
>
> *Richard and Monica have broken up, while Chandler and the aggravating Janice have not, much to Joey's distress. He doesn't want to lose Chandler's friendship, on the other hand, he can't stand Janice. 'I wanna pull my arm off just so as I have something to throw at her,' he admits.*
>
> *Poor Monica is a total mess. Her friends try to help. And fail. And Joey tries to get along with Janice by spending some quality time with her … And also fails.*
>
> *Meanwhile Ross confesses his fantasies to Rachel and ends up wishing he hadn't.*
>
> *Sweet, sophisticated and still very funny.*
>
> [*Radio Times*, 28 June – 4 July 1997]

2 Look at this extract from *The Secret History* by the American writer, Donna Tartt. As you read through the passage answer the following questions. What kind of people are being described in the extract? What have these people done, and what do they feel about what they have done? What kind of atmosphere is the writer trying to convey?

> *The bolt turned. Francis stepped in from the dark hall. He was breathing hard, pulling with dispirited jerks at the fingertips of a glove.*
>
> *'Jesus, Henry,' he said. 'What a night.'*
>
> *I was out of his line of vision. Henry glanced at me and cleared his throat*
> 5 *quietly. Francis wheeled around.*
>
> *I thought I looked back at him casually enough, but evidently I didn't. It must have been all over my face.*
>
> *He stared at me for a long time, the glove half on, half off, dangling limply from his hand.*
>
> 10 *'Oh, no,' he said at last, without moving his eyes away from mine. 'Henry. You didn't.'*
>
> *'I'm afraid I did.' Henry said.*
>
> *Francis squeezed his eyes tight shut, then reopened them. He had got very white, his pallor dry and talcumy as a chalk drawing on rough paper. For a moment I*
> 15 *wondered if he might faint.*
>
> *'It's all right,' said Henry.*
>
> *Francis didn't move.*
>
> *'Really, Francis,' Henry said, a trifle peevishly, 'it's all right. Sit down.'*
>
> *Breathing hard, he made his way across the room and fell heavily into an*

20 *armchair, where he rummaged in his pocket for a cigarette.*
'He knew,' said Henry, 'I told you so.'
Francis looked up at me, the unlit cigarette trembling in his fingertips.
'Did you?'
I didn't answer. For a moment I found myself wondering if this was all some
25 *monstrous practical joke. Francis dragged a hand down the side of his face.*
'I suppose everybody knows now,' he said. 'I don't even know why I feel bad
about it.'
Henry had stepped into the kitchen for a glass. Now he poured some Scotch in it
and handed it to Francis. …
30 *'Good Lord,' he said, and took a long drink. 'What a nightmare. I can't imagine*
what you must think of us, Richard.'
'It doesn't matter.' I said this without thinking, but as soon as I had, I realized,
with something of a jolt, that it was true; it really didn't matter that much, at least
not in the preconceived way that one would expect.
35 *'Well, I guess you could say we're in quite a fix,' said Francis, rubbing his eyes*
with thumb and forefinger. …
'Jesus,' he said to me. 'You're being so nice about this. I feel awfully embarrassed
about this whole thing.'
There was a long silence.
40 *Finally I said: 'What are you going to do?'*
Francis sighed. 'We didn't mean to do anything,' he said, 'I know it sounds kind
of bad, but what can we do about it now?'
The resigned note in his voice simultaneously angered and distressed me. 'I don't
know,' I said, 'Why for God's sake didn't you go to the police?'
45 *'Surely you're joking,' said Henry dryly.*
'Tell them you don't know what happened. That you found him lying out in the
woods. Or, God, I don't know, that you hit him with the car, that he ran out in
front of you or something.'

[Donna Tartt, *The Secret History*, Penguin, 1993]

Look at the following sentences taken from the text. What ellipses are present
here? The first has been done for you:

You didn't. (lines 10–11) means *You didn't tell him what we have done, did you?*
I'm afraid I did. (line 12)
He knew. (line 21)
Did you? (line 23)
I suppose everybody knows now. (line 26)
What are you going to do? (line 40)
I don't know. (lines 43–44)
Surely you're joking. (line 45)

How does the difference in meaning between *so* in line 21, and *so* in line 37 fit
in with what you have looked at earlier in this chapter?

Look again at the paragraph between lines 32 and 34. The author seems to be
playing around with the meaning of *it* here. What are those meanings? What is
it that matters here, and in what way does *it* not matter? Does it matter what
they have done, or what Richard feels about what they have done? How does
the use of *it* and *this* in this paragraph fit in with what you have looked at
earlier in this chapter?

While you were reading this passage you were thinking about the kind of atmosphere that the passage had conveyed. Think about your answers to the above questions, in the light of the atmosphere of the passage. How do the use of ellipsis, substitution and demonstratives contribute to that atmosphere?

WRITING ACTIVITY F

Read the following 'mini-saga':

THE PURSUIT OF YOUTH
The blonde and her
young student lover lived
together in his bedsitter.
She regarded the mirror
and worried. With fear in
her heart, she shopped every
lunch-hour, until their
room was stacked with lipsticks,
shoes and dresses.
One evening, opening the
wardrobe, she failed to see
his suit was gone.

[Suzi Robinson, *The Book of Mini-sagas*, Alan Sutton Publishing, 1985]

1 In pairs, write down ten questions that you would need to ask to find out, first, about the blonde and then the young lover. For example: 'How old was she?', 'How old was he?', 'What was her job?', 'What did his parents think about the relationship?', 'What did his friends think about the relationship?', 'Who did the cleaning, ironing, shopping, etc., in the relationship?'

2 Now go through the questions and write your own answers to them.

3 Imagine the scene at work when the blonde arrives tearful and bleary-eyed, having discovered that her lover has left. Now write down the conversation that two of her colleagues – one male and one female – have about the blonde and her situation.

4 Go through the conversation and work out where you have used ellipsis, and also where else you could use ellipsis.

2.4 Connectives

Look at this joke:

This woodcutter was walking through a wood with his axe looking for a tree to chop. Then he found one and he lifted up his axe and the tree said, 'Please, not me, please, I've got a wife and kids.'

So the woodcutter said, 'All right,' and he put down his axe and he went on his way.

And the tree turned to the tree next to him and he said, 'There goes a good feller.'

[*The Bumper Book of 3001 Jokes*, Cliveden Press, 1989]

Now, go through the joke again and think about how most of the sentences begin.

Most of the sentences in the above text begin with some kind of **connective**: *then, so, and*.

Connectives are words that are used to connect specific parts of a text. They are usually divided up into four different types, for the four different jobs that they do:

- **'And' connectives** – for example: *and, furthermore, for instance*.
- **'But' connectives** – for example: *but, however, instead, on the other hand*.
- **Cause connectives** – for example: *so, consequently, because, that being so*.
- **Time connectives** – for example: *then, next, at this moment, finally*.

2.4.1 'And' connectives

These normally introduce new information. In the joke about the woodcutter, the *And* at the beginning of the sentence moves you from one set of participants in the text to another set of participants.

'And' connectives also introduce examples and comparison. Look at the connectives at the beginnings of these sentences:

> *Anthropologists have brought us accounts of ways of life, in the far north, in the fastnesses of central India, or on remote Pacific atolls, which are so different from our own as to demonstrate how flexible human nature can be.*
>
> *For instance, there are the Dobuans, living on a small island off the southern coast of New Guinea, who are 'lawless and treacherous. Every man's hand is against every other man.' … Similarly, the Mundugamor families of northern New Guinea live in fortified solitude, the 'have-nots' raiding and attempting to rob the 'haves'.*
>
> [adapted from Dr Howard Jones, *Human Relationships and Group Behaviour*,
> James Clarke, 1963]

ACTIVITY 18

1 What is the writer of the above text doing with the Dobuans and the Mundugamor people? What is the job of a word like *similarly*? Could you rewrite the two paragraphs using any of the words that you looked at in Section 2.1.5?

Look at the joke about the woodcutter and the passage about the Dobuans and the Mundugamor. Who is likely to read these two texts? What are the differences in tone between the two texts? What are the differences in the types of 'and' connectives in each text? Given the audience and the tone of the texts, why are these different types of connectives being used?

The kinds of difference that you have just looked at are important when we look at other types of 'and' connective: in particular, terms such as *furthermore, in addition, besides, moreover, as well as*. Where are these words placed in the sentence? You can see from their positions in the sentence that they are used to emphasise addition. Could you use those words to replace the 'and' connectives in the woodcutter joke – and if not, why not?

2 The following are generally considered to be 'and' connectives. Go through
   them and put them into groups. Give each group a title that sums up the job
   that the connectives in that group do:

   *furthermore, incidentally, similarly, for instance, to summarise, again, in addition,
   by the way, actually, in conclusion, moreover, likewise, with reference to, really,
   besides, as well as, to summarise, for example, particularly, in the same way, then.*

2.4.2 'But' connectives

As you might imagine, 'but' connectives suggest that what follows them is
different from, or contrasted with, what comes in front of them.

▷ The following text has two 'but' connectives. What are they?

   *Critics should never imagine that they are powerful, but it would be culpable of them
   not to realise that they are bound to be influential. There is no reason, however, to be
   crushed flat by the responsibility of the job. It is, after all, a wonderfully enjoyable one.*

   [Clive James, *Visions Before Midnight,* Jonathan Cape, 1977]

In this text, the 'but' connectives are given additional emphasis by the
punctuation.

'But' connectives fall into two groups. The first group contains words that
suggest actual contrast: *conversely, instead, by contrast, in comparison, on the other
hand*. The second group contains words that show that the contrast is unexpected
or surprising. These words are often called 'concessive' connectors: *however, yet,
nevertheless, although, though, in spite of/despite that, all the same, even if.*

As you have seen above, the effect of these kinds of connectives is to make your
writing quite formal. This is often because writing down comparisons and
contrasts is quite an artificial exercise. Examination questions, for example, may
ask you to 'compare and contrast Y in terms of Z', but it would be unusual for
you to do this in a letter or in conversation.

The other point to notice is that there are two main ways of writing contrasts. In
the first pattern, the writer will usually make a generalisation, then list points
relating to Y, for example, and then make a list of points relating to X:

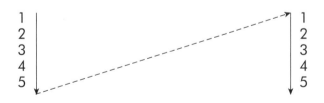

In the second pattern, the writer will usually compare and contrast Y and Z on a
point-by-point basis:

ACTIVITY 19
Read these two texts. Which text fits which pattern?

1   *Coal, gas and oil will eventually run out and other 'renewable' energy sources have their limitations. So, scientists have looked to nuclear energy which could provide all our needs. To some people, it's the future; to others, it's a world threat.*

   Supporters of nuclear-generated electricity argue that it is a relatively clean, safe, efficient way of making electricity. They say it causes less damage to the environment than burning fossil fuel; that more people die from air pollution caused by coal than from nuclear accidents or the small amounts of potentially dangerous radioactive waste produced by nuclear fission; and that only a tiny amount of raw uranium, compared to huge quantities of coal is needed to produce the same amount of electricity.

   However, campaigners against nuclear-generated electricity are worried about the potentially dangerous radioactive waste produced by nuclear power stations and the risk of accidents. They argue that high-level radioactive waste remains a threat to people for hundreds, possible thousands, of years so safe storage can't be guaranteed. They also argue that the accidents at Three Mile Island in America, in 1979, and Chernobyl in the Soviet Union, in 1986, prove that nuclear power isn't as safe as is claimed.

   [adapted from Lewis Bronze, Nick Heathcote and Peter Brown, *The Blue Peter Green Book*, BBC Books/Sainsbury's, 1990]

2   *Coal, gas and oil will eventually run out and other 'renewable' energy sources have their limitations. So, scientists have looked to nuclear energy which could provide all our needs. To some people, it's the future; to others it's a world threat.*

   Nuclear weapons may have prevented a world war. However, they still have the potential to destroy the world. Supporters of nuclear power say that nuclear power produces relatively small amounts of dangerous high-level radioactive waste which is stored safely. Opponents of nuclear power, on the other hand, say that nuclear power produces high-level radioactive waste which can be dangerous for thousands of years and nuclear weapons tests increase the amount of radiation in the atmosphere. It is true that nuclear power doesn't cause damaging acid rain, deadly air pollution or the green house effect. At the same time, it does produce low- and medium level radio active wastes and discharges which have increased radioactivity in the sea. Some people believe that nuclear power stations are relatively safe. However, their opponents say that nuclear power station accidents such as those at Three Mile Island and Chernobyl have killed people and are still affecting our environment in ways we have yet to fully understand.

   [adapted from Lewis Bronze, Nick Heathcote and Peter Brown, *The Blue Peter Green Book*, BBC Books/Sainsbury's, 1990]

Those writing about statistics and surveys tend to use the point-by-point pattern **2**, rather than pattern **1**. This kind of writing needs to be done quite carefully, or it can be rather boring and stodgy. You need to use both 'but' connectives and the ways of comparing and contrasting that we looked at in Section 2.1.5.

ACTIVITY 20

Look at the following extract from *The Sunday Times*. Underline all of the different kinds of words and phrases that create comparisons:

LOST BOYS: THE FACTS

- *By the year 2000 more women will be working than men.*
- *Two out of three women now work, 60% full-time.*
- *There are about 127,000 males aged 18–24 who have been unemployed for a year or more. Only 38,800 women fall in the same category.*
- *45.4% of women graduates are in work within six months of leaving university, as opposed to 42.3% of men. After a year 12% of male graduates are unemployed, but only 8% of women.*
- *Researchers predict that within a generation teaching will be an all-female profession.*
- *At school boys are lagging behind girls in all subjects, even in the sciences, the traditional 'male' preserve.*
- *In 1993 45.8% of girls achieved 5 top grade GCSEs (grades A, B, or C) compared with only 36.8% of boys.*
- *Girls are twice as likely to get an A in 'A' level English.*
- *Boys outnumber girls two to one in Britain's schools for children with learning difficulties. In special units for behavioural problems there are six boys for every girl.*
- *80% of girls plan to go on to college, compared with only 60% of boys.*
- *Young men represent one-eighth of the population but commit one-third of all crimes.*
- *The suicide rate among young men has risen by 70% in the last decade. Young men (15–24) have a suicide rate of 16 per 100,000: the rate for girls is five.*

[*The Sunday Times*, 2 April 1995]

WRITING ACTIVITY G

1 Look at the following list of statements about learning and education. Survey your friends and classmates. Ask them to what extent they agree with the statements on a scale of 1–5, where 1 means disagreeing and 5 means agreeing completely. Consider the results in terms of a number of variables; for example, whether the respondents are in education, whether they are planning to continue their education after the end of their present course, and their gender. Then write up your results into continuous prose.

   a People should be taught how to learn and then discover for themselves what they want to learn.
   b 'Those who can do, those who can't teach.'
   c Education is a life process and the needs of society are constantly changing. Therefore, formal education should not be packed into a few short years.
   d The role of education is to feed the mind, not the bank account.
   e As the need for unskilled labour declines, the demand for education will inevitably grow.
   f The prime role of education is to fulfil personal needs rather than those of greater society.

g Because children are full of natural, creative intelligence, education should be a joyful exploration of its potential.

h Since we can only reflect on the past and understand a little of our current situation, education cannot meet the demands of the future.

2 Look at the following table of the availability of certain durable goods in 1985 and in 1992. Write up the table into continuous prose, using the 'and' and 'but' connectives to show comparison and contrast.

Availability of Certain Durable Goods

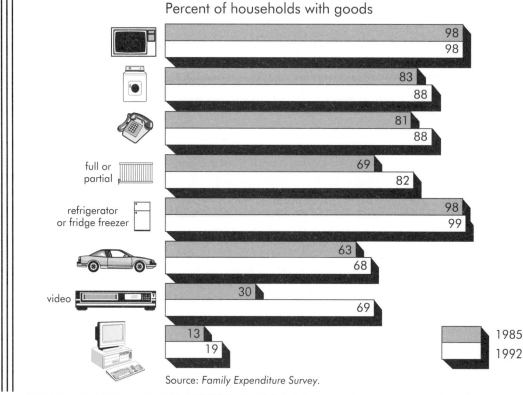

Source: *Family Expenditure Survey.*

2.4.3 Cause connectives

Read the following extract from Roger Hargreaves' *Mr Bounce* and decide why Mr Bounce wants to visit the doctor:

> *'This is ridiculous' Mr Bounce thought to himself, rubbing his head 'I must do something to stop all this bouncing about.'*
> *He thought and thought.*
> *'I know' he thought 'I'll go and see the doctor!'*
> *So, after breakfast, Mr Bounce set off to the nearest town to see the doctor.*
>
> [Roger Hargreaves, *Mr Bounce*, Thurman Publishing, 1976]

The answer to the question is very simple: to do something about all [his] bouncing about.

Now decide why Mr Bounce sets off to the nearest town. The answer is to see the doctor. The word that tells you this is *so*. In this passage there is a close relationship between 'causes' and 'consequences' or 'results'. Some connectives that signal this relationship are:

> *so, therefore, as a result, as a consequence, accordingly, consequently, thus, hence, for this/that reason*

These words are often preceded by *and*. We also use the word *because* to signal this relationship, although the meaning of *because* is subtly different, as we shall see.

ACTIVITY 21

Look at these excerpts from other Mr Men books. Before you read the extracts, decide what kind of audience the author, Roger Hargreaves, writes for. Which 'cause' connective does the author use? What is the relationship between the audience and the kind of 'cause' connective used?

> *Mr Greedy listened to what Doctor Plump had to say.*
> *'You'd like a Mr Skinny to come to stay?' he said.*
> *'To build up his appetite?' he added.*
> *'Delighted' he agreed.*
> *And so, Mr Skinny went to stay with Mr Greedy.*
> *He stayed for a month.*
> *And, during that, time, Mr Greedy did manage to increase Mr Skinny's appetite.*
> *And so, at the end of the month, Mr Skinny returned home.*
>
> [Roger Hargreaves, *Mr Skinny*, Thurman Publishing, 1978]

> *[Mr Busy] lived in a very busy-looking house which he'd built himself.*
> *As you can see.*
> *It had lots of doors and windows, and do you know what it was called?*
> *Weekend Cottage!*
> *Do you know why?*
> *Because that's how long it took him to build it!*
>
> [Roger Hargreaves, *Mr Busy*, Thurman Publishing, 1978]

> *'I've got one more idea' said Mr Robinson. 'I know somebody who writes children's books. Perhaps you could work for him?'*
> *So, the following day Mr Robinson took Mr Small to meet the man who wrote children's books.*
>
> [Roger Hargreaves, *Mr Small*, Thurman Publishing, 1972]

Deciding what is *cause* and what is *consequence* is not always easy. Look at this table:

Cause	Consequence
Mr Bounce wanted to see the doctor.	He set off for the nearest town.
Mr Skinny wanted to build up his appetite.	He went to stay with Mr Greedy.
Mr Greedy built up Mr Skinny's appetite.	Mr Skinny went home.
Mr Busy's house took a weekend to build.	The house is called Weekend Cottage.
Perhaps Mr Small could work for someone who writes children's books.	Mr Robinson took Mr Small to meet the man who wrote children's books.

If the sequence of events is 'cause' then 'result', the word used is *so*.

▷ Which other words from the above list can be used instead of *so*; in other words, which words from that list are **synonyms** for *so*?

Note that *so* and its synonyms can often be combined with *and*, as in the *Mr Skinny* extract.

ACTIVITY 22

Now read this extract from Charles Dickens' *The Old Curiosity Shop*. As you read it, note which 'cause' connective is used:

> *Now, the ladies being together under these circumstances, it was extremely natural that the discourse should turn upon the propensity of mankind to tyrannise over the weaker sex, and the duty that devolved upon the weaker sex to resist that tyranny and assert their rights and dignity. It was natural for four reasons: firstly, because Mrs. Quilp being a young woman and notoriously under the dominion of her husband ought to be excited to rebel; secondly, because Mrs. Quilp's parent was known to be laudably shrewish in her disposition and inclined to resist male authority; thirdly, because each visitor wished to show for herself how superior she was in this respect to the generality of her sex; and fourthly, because the company being accustomed to scandalise each other in pairs, were deprived of their usual subject of conversation now that they were all assembled in close friendship, and had consequently no better employment than to attack the common enemy.*

> [Charles Dickens, *The Old Curiosity Shop*]

1 In this passage which word is mostly used to show the 'cause/consequence' relationship; and which comes first – the 'cause' or the 'consequence'?

2 There is one main consequence, or result. What is it?

3 Another 'cause' connective is used in the passage. What is it?

4 Can you create a table such as the one given above to show the relationships between cause and result in the passage?

The use of *so* or its synonyms means that the 'cause' comes before the 'consequence' or 'result'. Using *because* means that you can choose to put the 'consequence' or 'result' before or after the cause. For example:

1 *Fabric nappies must be sterilized, washed and rinsed very thoroughly, because any traces of urine left on them will irritate your baby's skin and cause nappy rash.*

> [Elizabeth Fenwick, *The Complete Johnson and Johnson Book of Mother and Baby Care*, Dorling Kindersley, 1990]

or

2 *Because any traces of urine left on fabric nappies will irritate your baby's skin and cause nappy rash, they must be sterilized, washed and rinsed very thoroughly.*

Changing the sequence of 'cause' and 'consequence/result' changes the focus of the sentence.

▷ What is the difference in focus between **1** and **2** above?

ACTIVITY 23

Think carefully about the differences between the audiences for the Mr Men books, *The Complete Johnson and Johnson Book of Mother and Baby Care* and the works of Charles Dickens. What, do you think, is the relationship between the connectives used and the audience? What effect do the different kinds of connectives help to emphasize?

2.4.4 Time connectives

In the next section, you will look at the way we use certain words to organise text into stages.

ACTIVITY 24

Look at the following description of making bread in a factory.

1 Use this group of time connectives to put the sentences in the correct order: *first, second, then, after that, next, finally*. Put the time connectives at the beginnings of the sentences. What punctuation do you need?

   a _____ *the loaves have been baked, they are allowed to cool. Then they are wrapped in waxed paper to keep them fresh. Some loaves are cut into slices before being wrapped.*

   b _____ *the grain is sent to a flour mill, where it is ground into powdery flour. Sometimes chemicals are added to bleach the flour.*

   c _____ *combine harvesters cut the ripe cereal at harvest time, separating the grain from the stalks and husks. The combine harvester funnels the grain into a suitable container and leaves the straw behind in piles.*

   d _____ *lorries carry the loaves to shops.*

   e _____ *the flour goes to the bakery. There, the flour, the water, and the yeast mixture is made into dough. Sometimes, vitamins are added to increase the food value of the bread. A machine cuts the dough into loaf sized pieces.*

   f _____ *the loaves are placed in large room to rise. Then they are put into huge ovens that can bake hundreds of loaves at a time.*

   [adapted from C. J. Tunney and D. James (eds),
   New Junior Encyclopedia, Hamlyn, 1985]

2 Now match up the instructions with the following pictures:

You have just seen that time connectives are often used when piecing together a process. Note also the very common use of the passive form of verbs in description of processes.

Time connectives include all of the words that you have used above, as well as:

afterwards, subsequently, firstly, secondly, thirdly (etc.), finally, in conclusion, in the first place, to begin with, at last, in the end, eventually.

Time connectives can also be used in enumerating the parts of an argument:

As anyone with a younger brother or sister will know, most families now use disposable nappies. They make the whole business much easier. But there are four big problems with them. First, trees have to be cut down and turned to pulp which make the soft inside of each nappy. Second, to make the nappy look white, the pulp is bleached, possibly with chlorine which pollutes rivers. Third, a lot of each nappy is plastic, which is difficult to dispose of. Finally, used nappies take up a lot of space in landfill sites.

[Lewis Bronze, Nick Heathcote and Peter Brown, *The Blue Peter Green Book*, BBC Books/Sainsbury's, 1990]

Note that in this extract the passive is used in two particular sentences.

▷ When was it used, and why, do you think, it was used at those two points?

ACTIVITY 25

1 Read the extract from *The Old Curiosity Shop* again. Why has Dickens used 'time' connectives in this piece of writing? In situations like this, are such words really time connectives or do they have some other function? Is there a better name for these connectives in this kind of situation?

2 Look at some other descriptions of processes – particularly recipes, but also instructions for doing certain kinds of exercises. As you think about these descriptions, pay attention to their grammar. Do these descriptions use time connectives? If they don't use time connectives, why do you think that they don't?

WRITING ACTIVITY H

1 Write a description of a process that you know well, and as you write it use time connectives to sequence the description. Start with something simple, such as an exact description of boiling a kettle of water. Move on to something much more complicated, such as repairing a puncture in a bicycle tyre. These are only suggestions: choose something that you do, and then give your instructions to a friend and see if they can follow your instructions to complete the process themselves.

2 Use your instructions as part of a short leaflet aimed at young children. The leaflet should have the purpose of persuading young children to take up an activity.

3 Look, in a suitable textbook, for a pictorial description of a process; for example, the water cycle, paper-making or brewing. As you can see from the above extracts, children's encyclopaedias are good sources of these descriptions. Write the process out in continuous prose. Use time connectives where they are appropriate. Write the description for different audiences; first, for children of between 10 and 11 years old and, second, for people of your own age. How would the connectives be different?

3 Lexical cohesion

3.0 Introduction

In the previous chapter, we looked at how grammar works to hold texts together. In this chapter, we will be looking at the way in which words and their meanings hold texts together.

3.1 Repeated words

Read the following passage, which gives information on discipline standards in schools. As you read the passage, pick out all of the words that are repeated:

> *These are among the growing numbers of children who have been permanently or temporarily excluded from school. In the last school year, the number of permanently excluded or expelled totalled between 7,000 and 8,000 – against just 3,000 in 1990–91. Figures to be released shortly are expected to show that this school year is on course for an even more dramatic increase. As many as 90,000 pupils are now suspended each year for fixed periods.*
>
> *... Nor is the problem confined to older children. The most dramatic rise in exclusions in recent years has been in the primary sector. In Leicester, for example, figures published last month showed that the number of expulsions had trebled (from 74 to 201) in secondary schools since 1989 – but those in primary schools had increased fivefold (from six to 31).*

> [*Independent on Sunday*, 4 December 1994]

Some of the words you will have picked out are not words that deal with the theme of the passage. They are words such as *are, the, have, for, in,* and so on. We could find words like these in any passage with any theme. But there are three words that have to do with the theme of the passage: *excluded, expelled, suspended*. You can see that two of these words occur in the passage in two forms: *excluded/*

exclusion, expelled/expulsions. Although the word forms have changed, the words still connect to each other; they still have the same basic meaning, but the form of that meaning has changed slightly.

▷ Can you find another important word that is repeated in the passage?

Repeating words, even when they are repeated in slightly differing forms, is very important to the idea of cohesion. Repetition is a common device for holding text together. However, it is not good style to repeat too often.

In addition, repetition is **emphasis**.

ACTIVITY 26
What kind of text does the extract on school discipline come from? What do you think the purpose of the text is? Given that purpose, why would the writers of the text wish to use repetition in the way they do here? Do you think that these paragraphs come from towards the beginning or towards the end of the text?

Now look at the following text. As you read it, decide where you might find it and what its purpose is:

> **Are you in the know about Cheerios?**
>
> **The delicious, nutritious cereal with 4 different wholegrain O's**
>
> *You already know that Cheerios is the great-tasting cereal your whole family loves. But did you know it's the only cereal that combines four different wholegrain O's. The 4 different O's are made up of wholegrain corn, oats, rice and wheat.*

[Kelloggs Company]

▷ Which important words are repeated in the text and how do they hold the text together?
▷ What is the purpose of repetition in this kind of text?

ACTIVITY 27
Read the following passage. As you read it, decide what kind of text it is. What repetitions are made in this passage? (Don't forget the title here.) How do the repetitions make the text more coherent? What other purpose do these repetitions have? Apart from single words, what repetitions are there in the patterns of phrases?

> *THE CLOD & THE PEBBLE*
> *'Love seeketh not Itself to please,*
> *Nor for itself hath any care,*
> *But for another gives its ease*
> *And builds a Heaven in Hell's despair.'*
>
> > *So sang a little Clod of Clay*
> > *Trodden with the cattle's feet;*
> > *But a Pebble of the brook*
> > *Warbled out these metres meet:*
>
> *'Love seeketh only Self to please,*
> *To bind another to Its delight;*
> *Joys in another's loss of ease,*
> *And builds a Hell in Heaven's despite.'*

[William Blake, *Songs of Experience*]

WRITING ACTIVITY I

1 Collect up a number of examples of persuasive writing. Try to avoid the obvious categories of advertising; for instance, find examples of pamphlets and leaflets from organisations such as religious groups and political groups. What examples of repetition can you find in these texts? How and why is repetition used in these texts?

2 Using these texts as models, write a leaflet of your own that contains examples of repetition. Be careful that you pay attention to the other needs of writing a leaflet, such as layout, typography, pictures, and so on.

3.2 Synonyms

Look at the following passages. In each of them, there are words that have the same, or nearly the same, meaning. Here are some examples: *cried/weeping, rotting/decaying*.

▷ Can you find any others?

1 *Janine wanted to be pretty and have lots of friends, but instead she felt ugly and alone. Sometimes she cried for hours on her own, weeping because she thought she looked so awful that she couldn't go out.*

[Rosemary Conley, *Diet and Fitness*, August/September 1997]

2 **Hermit boy is rescued from home of squalor**
A tragic boy was kept a prisoner in his home amid the squalor of rotting animal carcasses. ...
Shocked police discovered the boy after breaking into his rundown home at New Haw, near Addlestone, Surrey.
They found him and his mother cowering in a bedroom littered with the decaying bodies of 28 dogs, cats, guinea pigs, hamsters, rabbits and birds.
Other live and unkempt animals scampered through the rubbish-strewn house scavenging for food.

[*Today*, 27 November 1991]

3 **Mystery of how seals find bank for holidays**
On the North Sea floor, off the Farne Islands, scientists have discovered a mysterious gathering place of grey seals.
It is the aquatic equivalent of a favourite country pub. Some seals will swim hundreds of miles through murky seas just to visit it.
The discovery has startled – and baffled – researchers who cannot explain why so many of these animals, from different colonies, continually head for this one tiny spot.
Nor can they explain how they navigate, flawlessly, through pitch-black water to reach a featureless 200ft-deep stretch of gravel.
'We have only just discovered that seals from different colonies head for this zone almost as if it were a magnet,' said Professor Mike Fedak, of the Sea Mammal Research Unit at St Andrews University.

[*The Observer*, 26 January 1997]

The words that you have picked out are generally called **synonyms**. One of the problems with synonyms is that it is very rare for different words to mean exactly the same thing.

ACTIVITY 28

1 Do you think that *crying* and *weeping*, from text **1** above, mean exactly the same thing? Do you think that *rotting animal carcasses* and *decaying bodies*, in text **2**, mean the same thing?

2 What kind of newspaper, do you think, contained text **3**? Why do you think that the journalists who wrote text **3** used the different phrases for the same thing? What impression were the journalists trying to create? What differences are there in the use of synonyms between the three extracts? How do you think those differences might be related to the different audiences for the three texts?

3 Now look at the following job advertisement. As you read through it, find the three different phrases that refer to the person required in the text:

> TEAM MEMBER (COMMUNITY SERVICES)
>
> *Phoenix House in partnership with Sheffield and Rotherham Association for the Care and Resettlement of Offenders (SARACRO) wish to appoint a community based outreach worker to provide counselling and support to SARACRO residents who may be experiencing substance use problems. The successful candidate will join a well established Community Services Team, based in Sheffield, and should have experience of working with substance users, young people and/or offenders. The role of the team member will be to: ...*

> [*The Guardian*, 29 January 1997]

What kind of text is this? Why do you think that *three different* phrases are used for the person required in the advertisement instead of the same phrase? Do the phrases all mean the same thing?

3.2.1 Register differences

What would have been the difference to text **3** above, from *The Observer*, if the journalists had used the word *boffin* instead of *scientists* or *researchers*? *Boffin* is a synonym for *scientist*, so why would it have been the wrong word in that text?

The answers lie in the idea of **register**. When we talk about register, we are talking about the relationship between a word and the social context in which it finds itself. The word *boffin* would have been wrong because it is too *informal*. A problem with trying to find synonyms is not that synonyms can't be found. The problem is that the word might not be the right word for that situation.

ACTIVITY 29

1 Think of the range of synonyms that there are for *toilet*. Order them in terms of formality in the following categories: taboo; slang/colloquial; informal; neutral; formal; very formal. What situations would be appropriate for the use of each word? Which people could you use those words with? More importantly, which people could you *not* use those words with?

Find synonyms for *drunk* and *mad*. These are words that have a wide range of synonyms which run through most of the register categories from 'taboo' to 'very formal'.

Think of some other nouns, adjectives or verbs, and see if they have synonyms that run through the register categories. Now think of the usual contexts of these words. What are the differences between words that have a wide register range and those that do not? For example, *toilet* has a wide range of synonyms, because society has many attitudes to the toilet and needs a wide range of synonyms to convey those attitudes. The word *scientist* doesn't have such a wide range of synonyms, because society doesn't have so many differing attitudes to scientists.

2　Take a number of reports of the same story from different newspapers. What synonyms do the different newspapers use for the same things? 'Human interest' stories are particularly good for this task.

WRITING ACTIVITY J

Change the register of the following texts by using synonyms for the important words. When you have done that, consider how appropriate the new register is. Is the new register appropriate or inappropriate? How does the idea of register influence your use of some words in some situations?

> *Every morning Mr Sneeze woke up, sneezed, got up, sneezed, got dressed, sneezed, went downstairs, sneezed, ate his breakfast, sneezed, and went to work, still sneezing.*
> [Roger Hargreaves, *Mr Sneeze*, World International Publishing, 1990]

> *Once upon a time there were three bears – Daddy Bear, Mummy Bear and little Baby Bear. They all lived together in a cottage in the wood. Every morning the three bears had porridge for breakfast. They each had their own bowl – a great big bowl for Daddy Bear, a medium-sized bowl for Mummy Bear, and a little baby bowl for little Baby Bear. One morning they sat down to eat their porridge and found it was too hot.*
> [*The Walker Book of Bear Stories*, Walker Books, 1995]

> *Sproggins had been an employee at the company of Smooth B'stard and Nephews for the duration of a year. In that time he had efficiently and discretely embezzled some five thousand pounds of the company's surplus emoluments. It was inopportune for Sproggins that for the duration of the preceding six months he had been under surveillance from a paid employee of the firm of P. Eye and Partners, surveillance agents. The ultimate crisis arose when Sproggins availed himself of the opportunity to purchase an automobile using bank notes specially treated with chemicals by Mr. Dick's employee.*

You will be considering register again in Section 3.7. In this section, you have been considering how choices of register prevent you from using certain words in certain situations.

3.3 Opposites

Words can also give a text cohesion because they are **opposites**. Unfortunately, this is not such a clear idea as it might at first seem. There are four different kinds of opposite:

- **Absolute opposites**. These kinds of opposites normally occur in pairs: for example – *dead/alive, present/absent, awake/asleep, male/female, even/odd (numbers), married/single*. These are opposites because they offer only two possibilities. Either you are awake or you are asleep; either a number is odd or it is even. Also, the negative of one of the pair is the synonym of the other, so that *not dead* is a synonym for *alive*.

- **Antonyms or gradable opposites**. These opposites also occur in pairs, but the choice here is not simply *either/or*. *Big* is opposite to *small*, but there is a scale from *big* to *small*. This is shown when we use words such as *quite* and *fairly* with these words; for example, *quite big*. Other examples of these are: *wide/narrow, fast/slow, happy/sad*.

- **Converseness or relational opposites**. These are also pairs, but they exist because of each other. An example of this is *parent/child*; if A is the *parent* of B, then – must be the *child* of A. Also, if A is the *teacher* of B, then – is the *pupil* of A. Other examples include: *give/receive, borrow/lend, buy/sell*.

- **Grouped opposites**. These occur when things in a text are mentioned in groups:

    Many of the world's sea creatures like seals, whales, dolphins, and porpoises are under threat because of the way we are treating them and their homes, the oceans.

    [Lewis Bronze, Nick Heathcote and Peter Brown, *The Blue Peter Green Book*, BBC Books/Sainsbury's, 1990]

The group is introduced by the phrase *many of the world's sea creatures*. This leads the reader to expect a group of things under this heading. But the individual things in the group are all different. The items in the group are not opposites in the sense that *alive* and *dead* are opposites. However, as we read the passage we expect to find contrasted and different things. The words act cohesively in the text in ways that are similar to the other opposites that we've just examined.

ACTIVITY 30
Read the following texts and decide which kind of opposites there are in each passage:

Keep unwanted animals out of your garden...
Visiting animals can prove a nuisance even in a well-fenced garden, but this clever gadget can chase them away using inaudible ultrasonic sound. Simply placed on a wall or post, the Ultrasonic Animal Chaser gives 24 hour protection from cats, dogs, rabbits, etc., in an area of up to 186sq m (2,000 sq ft).

[Innovations (Mail Order) plc, May–September 1997]

> *... but of this be sure,*
> *To do aught good never will be our task,*
> *But ever to do ill our sole delight,*
> *As being the contrary to his high will*
> *Whom we resist. If then his providence*
> *Out of our evil seek to bring forth good,*
> *Our labour must be to pervert that end,*
> *And out of good still to find means of evil; ...*

[John Milton, *Paradise Lost*, Book I, ll. 158–165]

'I bet,' said Wobbler, looking around, 'I bet ... I bet you wouldn't dare knock on one of those doors. I bet you'd hear dead people lurchin' about inside.'
  'Why do they lurch?'
  Wobbler thought about this.
  'They always lurch,' he said. 'Dunno why. I've seen them in videos. And they can push their way through walls.
  'Why?' said Johnny.
  'Why what?'
  'Why push their way though walls? I mean ... living people can't do that. Why should dead people do it?'

[Terry Pratchett, *Johnny and the Dead*, Corgi, 1994]

By this stage of the summer holidays, when boredom has probably replaced the excitement and novelty of 'no-school', your children may well be secretly wishing they were back at school with their friends.

[*The Asda Magazine*, August 1997]

Schools will normally arrange for you to discuss your child's assessment with teachers at a parents' meeting. At this meeting there will be a chance to discuss:

- *What the school has found out about your child's learning, and the next steps the teacher expects your child to take;*
- *How you can help your child; and*
- *When your next chance to discuss your child's progress will be.*

[*Qualifications and Curriculum Authority leaflet*]

Another problem with the idea of oppositeness is that some things in texts might seem to create a contrast that is hard to define.

In the following passage from his collection of stories, *Dubliners*, James Joyce suggests a contrast between Maria, who is a peace-maker, and the women around her, who are quarrelsome:

Maria was a very, very small person indeed, but she had a very long nose and a very long chin. She talked a little through her nose, always soothingly: 'Yes, my dear,' and 'No, my dear.' She was always sent for when the women quarrelled over their tubs and always succeeded in making peace. One day the matron had said to her:
  'Maria, you are a veritable peace-maker!'

[James Joyce, *Dubliners*, Penguin, 1956]

Notice here that we are using the word *contrast* instead of *opposite*. *Quarrelled* is not an **opposite** to *making peace*, but there is a definitely a contrast taking place. And the relationship between *quarrelled* and *a veritable peace-maker* is just as cohesive as the other opposite relationships that we have looked at.

ACTIVITY 31

Look at this excerpt from John Donne's poem 'A Valediction: forbidding Mourning'. As you read it, decide what contrasts Donne is trying to evoke. Think carefully here about the relationship between words and meaning:

> *As virtuous men pass mildly away,*
>   *And whisper to their souls, to go,*
> *Whilst some of their sad friends do say,*
>   *The breath goes now, and some say, no:*
>
> *So let us melt, and make no noise,*
>   *No tear-floods, nor sigh-tempests move,*
> *'T were profanation of our joys*
>   *To tell the laity our love.*
>
> *Moving of th' earth brings harms and fears,*
>   *Men reckon what it did and meant,*
> *But trepidation of the spheres,*
>   *Though greater far, is innocent.*
>
> *Dull sublunary lovers' love*
>   *(Whose soul is sense) cannot admit*
> *Absence, because it doth remove*
>   *Those things which elemented it.*
>
> *But we by a love, so much refined,*
>   *That our selves know not what it is,*
> *Inter-assured of the mind,*
>   *Care less, eyes, lips, and hands to miss.*

[John Donne, 'A Valediction: forbidding Mourning', in A. J. Smith (ed.), *John Donne: The Complete English Poems*, Penguin, 1971]

3.4 Superordinates

In the previous section, you were introduced to the idea of grouped opposites. The example that you were given was the following text:

> *Many of the world's sea creatures like seals, whales, dolphins, and porpoises are under threat because of the way we are treating them and their homes, the oceans.*
> [Lewis Bronze, Nick Heathcote and Peter Brown, *The Blue Peter Green Book*, BBC Books/Sainsbury's, 1990]

You knew that the grouped opposites were *seals, whales, dolphins, and porpoises*. You were also given a title for this group, and that title was *sea creatures*. You can see that *seals, whales, dolphins, and porpoises* are all kinds of *sea creatures. Sea creatures* is a more general term for *seals, whales, dolphins, and porpoises*.

There are two rather technical words for these items:

- *Sea creatures* is a **superordinate** term.
- *Seals, whales, dolphins, and porpoises* are all **hyponyms** of the superordinate *sea creatures*. Sometimes they are called **co-hyponyms**.

You can see, I hope, that the 'grouped opposites' are in fact, usually, co-hyponyms.

ACTIVITY 32

Look at the following texts. What is the superordinate and what are its hyponyms in each text?

> ***Keep unwanted animals out of your garden...***
>
> *Visiting animals can prove a nuisance even in a well-fenced garden, but this clever gadget can chase them away using inaudible ultrasonic sound. Simply placed on a wall or post, the Ultrasonic Animal Chaser gives 24 hour protection from cats, dogs, rabbits, etc., in an area of up to 186sq m (2,000 sq ft).*
>
> [Innovations (Mail Order) plc, May–September 1997]

> *The Bees of Death are big and black, they buzz low and sombre, the keep their honey in combs of wax as white as altar candles. Their honey is black as night, thick as sin and sweet as treacle.*
>
> *It is well known that eight colours make up white. But there are also eight colours of blackness, for those that have the seeing of them, and the hives of Death are among the black grass in the black orchard under the black-blossomed, ancient boughs of trees that will, eventually, produce apples that … Put it like this … probably won't be red.*
>
> [Terry Pratchett, *Eric*, Corgi / Victor Gollancz, 1990]

3.4.1 Meronyms, or part–wholes

Terry Pratchett's 'Bees of Death' text continues like this:

> *The grass was short now. The scythe that had done the work leaned against the gnarled bole of the pear tree. Now Death was inspecting his bees, gently lifting combs in his skeletal hands.*
>
> *A few bees buzzed around him. Like all beekeepers Death wore a veil. It wasn't that he had anything to sting, but sometimes a bee would get inside his skull and buzz around and give him a headache.*
>
> [Terry Pratchett, *Eric*, Corgi / Victor Gollancz, 1990]

The text describes a scene in an orchard. Not only are we told that there are trees in the orchard, but we are also given the names of parts of the trees: *blossom, bole, bough*. There is a **meronymic**, or **part–whole**, relationship between these words and the word *tree*. The extract contains other part–whole relationships: *hive/comb* and *skeleton/skull*. These relationships add to the cohesion of the text. They help to give us a very clear picture of the situation.

ACTIVITY 33

1 Look at the following texts and find examples of superordinates and meronyms:

> **8.00 Crime Beat**
>
> *CCTV at Work. The penultimate programme in the crime-prevention series looks at closed-circuit television's role in stamping out crime in towns and cities. Also, how the smoke barrier alarm is helping to combat computer thefts. Presented by Martin Lewis.*
>
> [*Radio Times*, 28 June – 4 July 1997]

> *A little lamp with a white china shade stood upon the table and its light fell over a photograph which was enclosed in a frame of crumpled horn. It was Annie's photograph. Little Chandler looked at it, pausing at the thin tight lips. She wore the pale blue summer blouse which he had brought her home as a present one Saturday. It cost him ten and elevenpence; but what an agony of nervousness it had cost him! How he had suffered that day, waiting at the shop door until the shop was empty, standing at the counter and trying to appear at his ease while the girl piled ladies' blouses before him, paying at the desk and forgetting to take up the odd penny of his change, being called back by the cashier, and finally, striving to hide his blushes as he left the shop by examining the parcel to see if it was securely tied.*
>
> [James Joyce, *Dubliners*, Penguin, 1956]

2 Look at all of the texts in this section. Which comes first in each text – the superordinate or the hyponym? Why does the hyponym come before the superordinate? Is this true of the part–whole relationship?

3.5 General nouns and text nouns

3.5.1 General nouns

There is a group of words that are used to refer generally to things, people or ideas. In general, this group is thought of as being a closed set of words, although there are some problems with this view, as we shall see in the next section.

● Humans – *people, person, man, woman, child, boy, girl*:

> *Eskimos. These* people *live in the far north of Canada and in Greenland. They also came from Asia, but later than the Indian.*
>
> [C. J. Tunney and D. James (eds), *New Junior Encyclopedia*, Hamlyn, 1985]

▷ Which people?

> *Boys learn from an early age that naughty is nice. It begins in the delivery room. 'What a big, handsome boy,' cries the midwife, when you know a girl would get 'Ah, how sweet'. When he headbutts a friend's front teeth or flatly refuses to stop turning the telly on and off, what is granny's reaction? 'Oh well,* boys *will be* boys.'*
>
> [*The Observer*, 26 January 1997]

▷ Which boys?

- Animals – *creatures*:

    Turning a corner we came upon a herd of dinosaurs. We crawled beneath them, aware of the size of their bulk above us. At one point I felt a scaly tail scrape along my back. Yet it did not seem at all strange that these prehistoric creatures had survived in this remote region.

    [adapted from a dream reported in A. Maley, *Short and Sweet*, Penguin, 1995]

    ▷ Which creatures?

- Countable inanimate nouns – *thing, object*:

    Raindrops on roses and whiskers on kittens,
    Bright copper kettles and warm woollen mittens,
    Brown paper packages tied up with strings,
    These are a few of my favourite things.

    Cream coloured ponies and crisp apple strudels,
    Door-bells and sleigh-bells and schnitzel with noodles,
    Wild geese that fly with the moon on their wings,
    These are a few of my favourite things.

    [Richard Rodgers and Oscar Hammerstein II,
    Williamson Music Co./Chappell & Co., 1959]

    ▷ Which things?

    A cigarette that bears a lipstick's traces,
    An airline ticket to romantic places,
    And still my heart has wings –
    These Foolish things remind me of you.

    [Holt Marvell, Jack Strachey and Harry Link, Boosey and Co. Ltd.,
    copyright renewed 1982]

    ▷ Which things?

- Uncountable inanimate nouns – *stuff*:

    Jill had left all of that curry in the pans. It was mouldy so I threw the stuff away.

    ▷ Which stuff?

    Ah, were I courageous enough
        To shout Stuff your pension!
    But I know, all too well, that's the stuff
        That dreams are made on: …

    [Philip Larkin, 'Toads', *Collected Poems*, Faber, 1988]

    ▷ How does Larkin use the two meanings of *stuff* for poetic effect here?

- Abstract nouns – *business, affair, matter*:

    ### Hider in the House
    11.25pm–2.15pmC4

    Until it breaks down the believability barrier, director Matthew Patrick's unusual psycho thriller is tightly constructed and grippingly well written. Former mental institution inmate Gary Busey hides in the home of well-to-do Mimi Rogers and Michael Mckean, obsessively spies on them and eventually intervenes in their personal affairs. Very creepy.

[*Radio Times*, 28 June – 4 July 1997]

▷ Which affairs?

Note also the use of the words *business, matter, affair* in phrases such as *a sorry business, the whole sorry affair, a bad business*, and so on. Like *idea* below, these words – *business, matter* and *affair* – are often part of a comment on the value of something.

● Action – *move*:

We came back from Japan and I got a job in Huddersfield. It seemed a good move at the time but now I'm not so sure.

▷ Which move?

● Place – *place*:

*This graveyard on the brink of Beeston Hill's
The place I may well rest if there's a spot
Under the rose roots and the daffodils
By which dad dignified the family plot.*

[from 'v.' by Tony Harrison, *Selected Poems*, Penguin, 1987]

And then me dad died and the house has been a sad place ever since.

▷ Which places?

● Fact – *idea*:

*One night when Nala was trying to fall asleep, she noticed the little lights of fireflies flying around her. She liked the way they made patterns in the air. The fireflies flew away and Nala decided to follow them.
    The jungle was very dark and scary. 'Maybe this wasn't such a good idea.'*

[*Disney and Me*, issue 153, 23 September 1997]

He said he wanted to throw up his course at college and go round the world. I told him that I thought it was a bad idea and he'd regret it for the rest of his life.

Note here that *idea* is often used with the words *good* and *bad*; that is, it is often part of a comment.

Sometimes these terms are changed around to give a comic effect.

▷ How is Lewis Carroll playing with general nouns in the following extract?

Alice caught the baby with some difficulty, as it was a queer-shaped little creature, and held out its arms and legs in all direction, 'just like a star-fish', thought Alice. The poor little thing was snorting like a steam-engine when she caught it, and kept doubling itself up and straightening itself out again, so that altogether, for the first minute or two, it was as much as she could do to hold it.

[Lewis Carroll, *Alice's Adventures in Wonderland*]

3.5.2 Text nouns

There is a group of words – quite a large group, in fact – that we use in writing to summarise information that we have just been given, or to point to what is to come

Look at the following text. As you read it, decide what kind of text it is.

▷ What do the words *situation* and *crisis* refer to?

> *In 1973 an international disaster was declared in the Sahelian countries of West Africa (Mauritania, Senegal, Mali, Upper Volta, Niger and Chad). It was reported that since 1968 there had been six years of drought, that most of the livestock were dead, and that the Sahelian population – numbering six million people – were in danger of starving to death. This* crisis *was identified and publicised by the Sahelian governments and by the Food and Agriculture Organisation of the United Nations (FAO). As the year went by they were joined by various international charities and relief organisations. A typical appeal went as follows:*
>
> *'The* situation *in the drought stricken Sahel region of Africa is almost impossible to grasp … Most of the cattle are dead anyway. Of thirst, starvation and disease. 100,000 human beings died of the same horrifying causes last year. Without help, God knows how many of the six million survivors will survive another year.'*

[adapted from Patrick Marnham, *Nomads of the Sahel*,
Minority Rights Group, 1979; emphasis added]

You can see, I hope, that *crisis* refers back to the information that you have read in the previous sentence. It is true that *crisis* does actually describe the terrible situation on the ground in which the people find themselves. But it is also a larger term, used to create the emotion around that situation and to report the situation in the text. In the second paragraph, *situation* is used to refer forward to the information that you are given in the other sentences in that paragraph.

These kinds of words are very important in factual writing. This is often because the words contribute a great deal to the density and 'importance' of the text.

Now read the following passage.

▷ What kind of text is it?
▷ The text noun here is the word *trend*. Which facts does it refer back to in the text?

> *One example of the multicultural society we live in is the number of people involved in mixed-race relationships. The 1991 Census found that Black men are the most likely of any ethnic group to be married to or living with people of different ethnic origin. Over 30 per cent of Black men aged 16–24 and in a stable relationship are living with a White partner, compared with 23 per cent of Black women and 1 per cent of White men or women. Although there are no earlier figures for comparison, it is widely believed this is an increasing* trend.

[*The Guardian*, 4 February 1997; note that, for the purposes of the article extracted
here, the terms 'Black' and 'White' were used when those involved chose to
describe themselves as such]

ACTIVITY 34

1 In the right-hand column below are definitions of the nine words in the left-hand column. Match the words with the definitions:

1 Fact

    a A state of affairs that you have just mentioned or are about to mention and suggest that it is true.

2 Issue

    b A subject that is not yet certain and is considered to be worth discussing.

3 Move

    c What is happening or likely to happen in connection with a particular matter, and which may be difficult or unpleasant.

4 Point

    d A particular fact or idea that is used in a discussion, argument or debate to persuade.

5 Problem

    e A situation or a state of affairs that causes difficulties for people, so that they try to think of a way to deal with it.

6 Question

    f A belief or opinion that you have on a particular topic.

7 Situation

    g An important subject that people are discussing or arguing about.

8 Trend

    h A general and obvious movement or development of events, fashion, attitudes, and so on.

9 View

    i A change in situation, attitude, policies, opinions, and so on.

See page 65 for the answers.

2 Now use the text nouns that you have just defined in the gaps in the following passage:

The (1)_____ of what should be done to relieve the problem of drought is one that has vexed many water boards over the last few months. Some think that water should be moved to parts of the country where there is a shortage. However, this (2)_____ is not widely shared and is very unrealistic. The (3)_____ is that there is water in the North of England and Scotland but the cost of transporting it to other parts of the country is too high. In addition, the water table in the South and South east of England has been low for the last two years. This (4)_____ shows no sign of abating. The Government has tried to force the water boards to fix leaking pipes, but this (5)_____, although laudable, has had little real effect. The (6)_____ that most politicians choose to ignore is that the unreasonable demand being made on our rivers and streams is an untenable (7) _____. The (8)_____ is that too much water is being used up in trivial ways, in car washes, dishwashers, etc., and no government knows best where to stand on this (9)_____ .

Again, see page 65 for the answers.

3 Here is another group of text nouns. Their definitions are in the right-hand column but they are not in the correct order. Match the nouns on the left with their definitions on the right:

1 Aspect	**a**	A discussion about a subject on which people have different views.
2 Decision	**b**	A set of statements in support of an opinion or a course of action, expressed in an orderly way and used to try to convince someone that the opinion or course of action is correct.
3 Argument	**c**	Something you decide is true as a result of knowing that other things are true.
4 Debate	**d**	A choice that you make about what you think should be done or about which is the best of various alternatives.
5 Conclusion	**e**	Something that you expect or know is going to happen.
6 Prospect	**f**	One way of considering something when there are many possible ways.

See page 65 for the answers.

[All definitions taken from the *Cobuild English Language Dictionary*, Collins, 1987]

You can see here, I hope, that these words are often used when a passage has a very high information content. Often, the passage contains a lot of formal English. There are many more words of this kind, and you should try to notice them as and when they occur.

WRITING ACTIVITY K
Write two or three similar paragraphs about a problem that you feel strongly about, using text nouns where appropriate.

3.6 Collocations

Let's return briefly to a newspaper text that you have looked at above. Here is the full version of the first six paragraphs of the passage. As you read it this time, pick out words that seem to have to do with (**a**) *being a prisoner* and (**b**) *filth and decay*:

Hermit boy is rescued from home of squalor
A tragic boy was kept a prisoner in his home amid the squalor of rotting animal carcasses.

The 11-year-old was rarely allowed out, never attended school and banned from speaking to neighbours.

Shocked police discovered the boy after breaking into his rundown home at New Haw, near Addlestone, Surrey.

They found him and his mother cowering in a bedroom littered with the decaying bodies of 28 dogs, cats, guinea pigs, hamsters, rabbits and birds.

> *Other live and unkempt animals scampered through the rubbish-strewn house scavenging for food.*
>
> *Last night Chief Inspector Martin West said: "The mother appears to be as much in need of help as her son. They have been taken to a community home where they can be looked after."*

[*Today*, 27 November 1991]

The words that seem to go together are as follows:

a Being a prisoner: *rescued, prisoner, rarely allowed out, banned*. We could perhaps add the word *hermit* to this list, except that hermits are generally volunteers.

b Filth and decay: *squalor, rotting, rundown, littered, decaying, unkempt, rubbish-strewn*.

We can say, as we have done above, that some of the words are actually synonyms. We can also say that *animals* is a superordinate of the types of animals listed in paragraph 4 of the extract. However, we can't readily put the groups of words into any of the other word groupings that we have looked at above. We couldn't automatically say that the words in group **b** were, for example, all synonyms for *filth and decay*. But it is clear that the words are actually related in meaning. This relatedness in meaning adds immeasurably to the cohesion of the passage. We call the way in which these words connect to each other **collocation**.

ACTIVITY 35

Look at these first five verses from the poem 'v.' by the contemporary poet, Tony Harrison. The beginning of the poem describes a visit made by the poet to the graveyard where both his mother and his father are buried. As you read the extract pick out words which go together.

How easy is it to find words that go together? How is the effect of collocation in this poem different from the effects of the collocation in the piece of journalism in the previous text?

> *Next millennium you'll have to search quite hard*
> *To find my slab behind the family dead,*
> *Butcher, publican, and baker, now me, bard*
> *Adding poetry to their beef, beer and bread.*
>
> *With Byron three graves on I'll not go short*
> *of company, and Wordsworth's opposite.*
> *That's two peers already, of a sort,*
> *And we'll all be thrown together if the pit,*
>
> *Whose galleries once ran beneath this plot,*
> *Causes the distinguished dead to drop*
> *Into the rabblement of bone and rot,*
> *Shored slack, crushed shale, smashed prop.*
>
> *Wordsworth built church organs, Byron tanned*
> *Luggage cowhide in the age of steam*
> *And knew their place of rest before the land*
> *Caves in on the lowest worked-out seam.*

> *This graveyard on the brink of Beeston Hill's*
> *The place I may well rest if there's a spot*
> *Under the rose roots and the daffodils*
> *By which dad dignified the family plot.*
>
> [from 'v.', Tony Harrison, *Selected Poems*, Penguin, 1987]

WRITING ACTIVITY L

Choose a place you know well and that you feel that you can describe quite accurately, and write a description of it. (Alternatively, choose a person.) Write between 80 and 100 words. When you have finished, look at all of the words you have used that you feel 'collocate' together. Are there many collocations? Is it like the tabloid journalism of the 'hermit boy' text? Or are there rather fewer collocations, and is there a greater sense that you have used a wider vocabulary?

3.7 Formality and register

In the previous section we saw how words can be grouped. This happens because they are part of a subject matter. In Section 3.2, we looked at the way in which synonyms are influenced by the **formality** or otherwise of the context in which words are used. We are now going to look at how those two ideas can be brought together. We are going to see how levels of formality gather certain groups of words around them. We are then going to see how this idea of formality affects specialised areas of language.

Now read through the following text.

▷ Can you decide, roughly, when you think it was written?
▷ If you know when it was written and the name of the author, then can you pick out the words which, for you, make the language appropriate for that period and that writer?

> *'Mr. C,' returns Vholes, 'I wish to say no more of any third party than is necessary. I wish to leave my good name unsullied, together with any little property of which I may become possessed through industry and perseverance, to my daughters Emma, Jane and Caroline. I also desire to live in amity with my professional brethren. When Mr. Skimpole did me the honour, sir – I will not say the very high honour, for I never stoop to flattery – of bringing us together in this room, I mentioned to you that I could offer no opinion or advice as to your interests, while those interests were entrusted to another member of the profession. And I spoke in such terms as I was bound to speak, of Kenge and Carboy's office, which stands high. ...'*

It is quite clear that this is not language that we would hear anyone speaking these days. Although there are likely to be few words here that you have never heard before, the language is too formal for us at the end of the twentieth century. This scene takes place in a solicitor's office, and we all know that the language of the law is very formal. However, the language is formal even for a modern law office.

One of the things about formality is that it tends to show itself in 'older' English. This 'older' English is a combination of long words, usually of Latin origin, and long sentences. As I typed out the passage, my computer underlined the sentence *When Mr. Skimpole … of the profession.* with a wavy red underline, which means that the computer thought that the sentence was too long. However, it is important to note that the computer's grammar checker has been designed to check language at the end of the twentieth century.

The text is from Charles Dickens' novel, *Bleak House*, which was first published in 1852–53.

WRITING ACTIVITY M

Now read through the following text, which was written about 25 years after *Bleak House*. Rewrite it so that it is in a more modern, less formal style. As you think about the rewriting, think particularly about the vocabulary, but also about making the sentences less formal and slightly looser. It may help to think of someone you know now who might be like this person.

> Joshua Brookes, as second master, presided over the middle school, and surely never
> M.A. had so thankless an office. He was placed at a terrible disadvantage in the
> school, not altogether because he had risen from its lowest ranks – not altogether
> because a drunken foul-mouthed cripple interfered with their sports, or went reeling
> to his son's domicile next door – not because he was unduly severe; other masters were
> that – but because his own eager thirst for knowledge as a boy had made him
> intolerant towards indolence, incredulous of incapacity; and his constitutional
> impatience and irritability made his harsh voice seem harsher when he reproved a
> dullard. He lost his self-command, and with that went his command over others.
>
> [Mrs Linnaeus Banks, *The Manchester Man*, 1876]

In some ways, this exercise is quite easy(!). It is relatively easy to modernise a text. The language of the past can often seem distant, and easy to move away from.

However, when it comes to legal writing, rewriting in the way you have just done is very hard – the formality is built in. Look at this example from a contract for a pension scheme:

> I declare that the total contribution to be paid by me on my behalf, together with
> contributions paid to retirement annuity contracts or trust schemes and any other
> personal pension schemes by me or on my behalf do not exceed the maximum
> permitted by the Inland Revenue. I further declare that the contributions paid by me
> or on my behalf are not in respect of emoluments received as a controlling director of
> an investment company (Income and Corporation Taxes Act 1988 Section 644(5)) nor
> in respect of emoluments to which Section 644 (6A) of the Income and Corporation
> Taxes Act 1988 applies.
>
> [Scottish Amicable Personal Pension document Y720/1/96]

Again, my computer has put a wavy red line under that last sentence. We could try to change some of the words. The *Shorter Oxford English Dictionary* defines *annuity* as 'An investment of money entitling the investor to a series of equal annual sums'; it also defines *emoluments* as 'Profit or gain arising from office or employment; reward, remuneration'. So perhaps we could put *retirement investment contracts*, instead of *retirement annuity contracts*. We could put *rewards received as a controlling director of an investment company*, instead of *emoluments received as a controlling director of an investment company*. But that would be just tinkering.

The thing with modern legal language is not just that it is formal, but that it is a self-contained language. It is a language used by a very few people in a particular profession. The insurance company that published the piece above would probably like to simplify it for their customers. However, their writing is scrutinised by the Inland Revenue service to make sure that it conforms to the language of the original writers of the law that the insurance company follows. Those writers are the legal writers who write the law passed by Parliament. There is a knock-on effect. Parliament writes law in a particular way. That writing forces the Inland Revenue to scrutinise the writing of the companies that are bound by that law. This kind of language area, created to suit a group of people in a particular situation, is what is known as a **genre**. Confusingly, you will also find that a genre is sometimes also called a 'register'.

ACTIVITY 36

Read the next extract. There is a gap in the middle of it. Fill that gap with the word that you think fills it the best:

> *Theft-deterring deadlocking is standard on virtually all _____ across the range, as are security-coded radios and visible vehicle identification numbers located on the left at the top of the dash panel.*

You may have chosen a word such as *car*, or possibly *vehicle*. But it would have been relatively easy to choose a word, because all of the words around the gap belong to the language of motor vehicles. We could go even further and say that the language in the extract is that of motor-vehicle security.

> [The extract is from Vauxhall's Index publication, sheet P97 3/96 entitled Vauxhall Security.]

ACTIVITY 37

1 Read the following three texts. As you do so, decide which area of language – which **genre** – they are from. As you make your decisions, work out how you came to those decisions:

> 1. *Remove band tightening screw, by gently pulling the end of the bracket band. Unthread the band.*
> 2. *Wrap the band around the handlebar and rethread. Ensure the final position does not interfere with any moving part or brake or gear cable.*
> 3. *Pull the band to tighten and reinsert the band tightening screw.*
> 4. *Turn band tightening screw with flat head screw driver to ensure a secure fit.*
> 5. *Adjust the angle of the light by loosening the adjustment screw and retightening when in the desired position.*
> 6. *Slide the front light down until locked into the bracket.*

> *Even with a simple presentation, it is worth sparing a moment or two to make it look attractive. Sprinkle with fresh herbs, chopped toasted nuts or grated orange and lemon rind. For extra flavour, toss the cooked vegetables in a little fruit juice or shoyu, or a mixture of shoyu and tahini.*

> *Skipper Mike Ainsworth, who was also captain of the Navy side, plumped for me in favour of Jim Pressdee, the Glamorgan player, and I am glad to say that I repaid his*

confidence by scoring 22 and 66, though we were not unnaturally outplayed by the tourists. Early in the Australian innings, Keith Miller pushed a possible catch straight through the legs of the rather portly Major Parnaby, who was fielding at short leg.

[Extracts, in order: from instructions accompanying an L.E.D. Safety Light Set, for a cycle; Sarah Brown, *Sarah Brown's Vegetarian Cookbook*, Grafton Books, 1986; Colin Ingleby-Mackenzie, *Many a Slip*, Oldbourne, 1962]

2 Collect examples of writing from different genres. Type them up on different sheets of paper and show them to fellow students to see if they can guess what the genres of the pieces are.

The fun starts, of course, when writers mix registers and use the language of one register in a completely different context. You can see this in the e. e. cummings poem that we read in Chapter 2, and in this text from the beginning of a poem by Simon Armitage:

VERY SIMPLY TOPPING UP THE BRAKE FLUID

Yes, love, that's why the warning light comes on. Don't
panic. Fetch some universal brake-fluid
and a five-eighths screwdriver from your toolkit
then prop the bonnet open. Go on, it won't

eat you. Now, without slicing through the fan-belt
try and slide the sharp end of the screwdriver
under the lid and push the spade connector
through its bed, go on, that's it. Now you're all right

to unscrew, no, clockwise, you see it's Russian
love, back to front, that's it. You see, it's empty.

[Simon Armitage, *Zoom*, Bloodaxe Books, 1979]

WRITING ACTIVITY N

1 Write a short paragraph using language from an area that you know well. Don't provide a title for it. Show your piece to some fellow students and see if they can guess the context for the writing.

2 Use the piece that you have just written and change it so that it is now in another genre. Use the Armitage poem as a guide. For example, you could take your piece of writing and turn it into cookery instructions, or tabloid journalism. Or you could take cookery instructions and turn them into a poem. For another example of instructions as poetry, look at Peter Porter's poem 'Your Attention Please'.

Answers to exercise on text nouns in Section 3.5

1 1 (Fact), a; 2 (Issue), g; 3 (Move), i; 4 (Point), d; 5 (Problem), e; 6 (Question), b; 7 (Situation), c; 8 (Trend), h; 9 (View), f.

2 1, question; 2, view; 3, problem; 4, trend; 5, moves; 6, point; 7, situation; 8, fact; 9, issue. (You may feel that some, but not all, of these are interchangeable. However, are the items you want to interchange synonyms?)

3 1 (Aspect), f; 2 (Decision), d; 3 (Argument), b; 4 (Debate), a; 5 (Conclusion), c; 6 (Prospect), e.

4 Patterns in a text

4.0 Introduction

In the previous chapters, we have looked at how texts are held together or 'have cohesion' in two particular ways. First, we looked at the way in which some words hold the text together grammatically. Second, we looked at the way in which the meanings of words group them together. In this chapter, we are going to examine the way in which certain patterns occur – or, more correctly, re-occur – in texts. Some of these patterns occur in paragraphs: some, however, occur in much larger pieces of text.

4.1 General–specific patterns

Some of you will have been taught that a paragraph is a group of sentences about one thing, or one topic. Because of this idea, we often try to write topic sentences at, or near, the beginning of a paragraph. A topic sentence is a sentence that introduces the reader to the topic or subject of the paragraph. In this section we are going to look at this idea of a 'topic sentence' at, or near, the beginning of a passage. However, we are going to look at it from a slightly different point of view.

Read the following two paragraphs.

▷ What kind of text do the paragraphs come from?

> **Beatles, the** /biːtlz/ *English pop group 1960–1970. The members, all born in Liverpool, were John Lennon (1940–1980, rhythm guitar, vocals), Paul McCartney (1942–, bass, vocals), George Harrison (1943–, lead guitar, vocals), and Ringo Starr (formerly Richard Starkey 1940–, drums). Using songs written largely by Lennon and McCartney, the Beatles dominated rock music and pop culture in the 1960's. The Beatles gained early experience in Liverpool and Hamburg, West Germany. They*

had a top-30 hit with their first record, 'Love Me Do' 1962, and every subsequent single and album released until 1967 reached number one in the UK charts. At the peak of Beatlemania they starred in two films, A Hard Day's Night 1964, and Help! 1965, and provided the voices for the animated film Yellow Submarine 1968. Their song 'Yesterday' 1965 was covered by 1,186 different performers in the first ten years. The album Sgt Pepper's Lonely Hearts Club Band 1967, recorded on two four-track machines, anticipated subsequent technological developments.

As you might have guessed, the text comes from an encyclopaedia.

[*The Hutchinson Encyclopedia*, Helicon Publishing, 1992]

We can see that the first part of the first paragraph introduces us to the subject of the text.

What would you think if you read a single statement that said **Beatles, the** /biːtlz/ *English pop group 1960–1970* and nothing more. Either you would think 'So what!', or you would think 'This isn't enough information. Tell me more.' The rest of the text 'tells you more'. You move from the 'general' to the 'specific'. Notice the way in which the subjects of the sentences are always the Beatles, or pronouns and words that refer explicitly to them: *the members, the Beatles, The Beatles, They, they, Their.* The subject of the final sentence is *The album*, but it could quite as easily have begun with *Their album*.

ACTIVITY 38

Now read another text from the same encyclopaedia. Which part of the text is general and which part is specific? How are the sentences in the specific part of the text linked to the general part?

> **bluestocking** *learned woman; the term is often used disparagingly. It originated 1750 in England with the literary gatherings of Elizabeth Vesey (1715–1791), the wife of an Irish MP, in Bath, and Elizabeth Montagu, a writer and patron, in London. According to the novelist Fanny Burney, the term arose when the poet Benjamin Stillingfleet protested that he had nothing formal to wear. She told him to come in his 'blue stockings' – that is, in ordinary clothes. The regulars of these gatherings became known as the Blue Stocking Circle.*
>
> [*The Hutchinson Encyclopedia*, Helicon Publishing, 1992]

But encyclopaedia entries are not the only places where you will find the general–specific pattern.

ACTIVITY 39

1 Look at the following passage. As you read it, decide what kind of text it comes from and what the functions of this passage are. For example, is it descriptive, narrative, informative or argumentative? How many general–specific patterns are there? Do the general parts always occur at the beginnings of the paragraphs? If they do not, why do you think they don't? In this text, how are the 'specifics' linked to the 'generals'?

> *For the first time since the storm reached its height they could see the ship from one end to the other. For the first time they saw the gaping crater left by the funnel's roots. Smashed derricks, knotted stays. The wheelhouse, like a smashed conservatory. The list, too, of the ship: that had been at first a thing felt: then, as*

they grew accustomed to it, almost a thing forgotten; but now you could see the horizon tilted sideways, the whole ocean tipped up at a steep slope as if about to pour over the edge of the world: so steep that it seemed to tower over the lee-bulwarks. It was full of sharks, too, which looked at you on your own level – or almost, it seemed from above you. It looked as if any moment they might slide down the steep green water and land on the deck right on top of you. They were plainly waiting for something: and waiting with great impatience.

But the sharks were not the only living things. The whole ruin of the deck and upper-structures was covered in living things. Living, but not moving. Birds, and even butterflies and big flying grasshoppers. The tormented black sky was on incessant flicker of lightning, and from every mast-head and derrick-point streamed a bright discharge like electric hair; but large black birds sat right amongst it, unmoving. High up, three john-crows sat on the standard compass. A big bird like a crane, looking as if its wings were too big for it when folded up, sat on a life boat, staring through them moonily. Some herons even tried to settle on the lee-bulwarks, that were mostly awash; and were picked like fruit by the sharks. And the birds like swallows: massed as if for migration. They were massed like that on every stay and hand rail. But not for migration. As you gripped a hand-rail to steady yourself they never moved; you had to brush them off: when they just fell.

The decks were covered in a black and sticky oil, that had belched out of the funnel. Birds were stuck in it, like flies on a fly-paper. The officers were barefoot and as they walked they kept stepping on live birds – they could not help it. I don't want to dwell on this, but I must tell you what things were like, and be done with it. You would feel the delicate skeleton scrunch under your feet: but you could not help it, and the gummed feathers hardly even fluttered.

[Richard Hughes, *In Hazard*, Chatto and Windus, 1938]

2 Read the following passage from E. M. Forster's *A Room with a View*. As you read it, decide what the purpose of the passage is. Then look at the passage in terms of a general–specific pattern.

Secrecy has this disadvantage: we lose the sense of proportion; we cannot tell whether our secret is important or not. Were Lucy and her cousin closeted with a great thing which would destroy Cecil's life if he discovered it, or with a little thing which he would laugh at? Miss Bartlett suggested the former. Perhaps she was right. It had become a great thing now. Left to herself, Lucy would have told her mother and her lover ingenuously, and it would not have remained a little thing. 'Emerson, not Harris': it was only that a few weeks ago. She tried to tell Cecil even now when they were laughing about some beautiful lady who had smitten his heart at school. But her body behaved so ridiculously that she stopped.

[E. M. Forster, *A Room with a View*, Penguin, 1990]

What is the relationship between the general–specific pattern, and the purpose of the part of the text that you have read?

WRITING ACTIVITY O

Look at these two property descriptions from estate agents' brochures. As you read them, pick out the general–specific pattern in the text.

1 *A fine inner through semi-detached house situated in a main road town location convenient for bus and train services, local schools and approx. 1 mile from the town*

centre. The property has established gardens both front and rear, and a solid fuel central heating system. The accommodation briefly comprises vestibule, lounge-dining room, kitchen, 3 1st floor bedrooms, and bathroom.

2 *A grade II listed detached cottage situated in a pleasant cul-de-sac rural location. The property has well-stocked gardens to front and rear, with parking area to the rear. The accommodation briefly comprises lounge, dining room, kitchen, ground floor bathroom, 4 1st floor bedrooms, and a 1st floor bathroom.*

Now write a description of your own house or flat, using these two texts as models.

4.2 Cause–consequence patterns

In Section 2.4, we looked at the way in which words and phrases such as *because, so, as a result of, consequently* and *therefore* showed a 'cause–consequence' relationship between sentences. You will remember that cause–consequence relationships imply that *A causes B*, or that *B is the result of A*. Cause–consequence relationships are also possible across larger stretches of text.

ACTIVITY 40

Look at the following passage. It is taken from an autobiographical book that describes a child's upbringing in Romania in the early decades of the twentieth century. In this passage, the writer is describing some tricks that he and his friend, Wolf, played on the family's butler, Geib. As you read the passage, decide what the relationship is between the two young friends and the butler:

The horn on the car door bothered Wolf; he found it antiquated. And so for fun I took my slingshot and aimed at the rubber balloon; the sharp impact of the lead pellet made the copper horn beep short and loud. Geib, who happened to be working nearby, quickly unlocked the garage door, came in and carefully examined the entire automobile, more and more perplexed and puzzled as to who had honked.

This turned into a game, which entertained us as much as the slapstick scenes from the Buster Keaton and Harold Lloyd comedies which were all the rage then. If we knew that Geib or Haller was in the vicinity, I would shoot at the balloon, the honk inevitably summoned one or the other, and he would unlock the garage and comb every nook and cranny for the mysterious force that made the horn beep. Meanwhile, we lay well concealed behind the skylight trying to choke back our mirth. When the fruitless investigation was abandoned and the garage locked up again, I would take another shot and the mystification would begin again.

Once though, Haller found one of my lead pellets, which he was familiar with because I made them in his smithy. He put it in his pocket, and for a while we held back on our joke, waiting anxiously for the sequel. But nothing happened and we resumed our mischief. I became so audacious, especially with Old Geib, that I would shoot at the horn a second time the instant he turned away from the car, so that the blare at his back made him whirl around, as though the car were about to start by itself, honking at him to get out of the way.

[Gregor von Rezzori, *Memoirs*, Picador, 1981]

1   Go back through the passage and fill in the following table with the
    appropriate causes and consequences. Some are done for you:

    Causes   **Consequences**

    i   ...   **i**   ... the copper horn beeps...

    ii ...   **ii**   ... Geib came in and examined
                                                     the car.

    iii If Geib and Haller and near.   **iii** ...

    iv The garage is locked up.   **iv**   ...

    v   Haller finds one of the lead pellets.   **v**   ...

                                            vi   ...

2   Look carefully at the word *consequences* in the final paragraph of the passage.
    What is the cause of the consequences that they wait for? Where does this fit
    into the table above? (There is actually a space for it.)

3   Now create your own grid for these excerpts from two Mr Men books, the first
    of which you have already seen before:

    Mr Greedy listened to what Doctor Plump had to say.
    'You'd like a Mr Skinny to come to stay?' he said.
    'To build up his appetite?' he added.
    'Delighted' he agreed.
    And so, Mr Skinny went to stay with Mr Greedy.
    He stayed for a month.
    And, during that time, Mr Greedy did manage to increase Mr Skinny's appetite.
    And so, at the end of the month, Mr Skinny returned home.
    Happy!
    With a tummy!
    A tummy was something Mr Skinny had always wanted.
    'I never knew I had it in me' he chuckled to himself.

    [Roger Hargreaves, *Mr Skinny*, Thurman Publishing, 1978]

    Poor Mr Happy had had a tiring day.
    Rushing here and there and back again cheering people up was hard work.
    'Phew' he sighed as he went into his house and sat down for a well-earned rest on
    a kitchen chair.
    But then, do you know what happened?
    It fell to bits.
    BUMP went poor Mr Happy.
    'That's all I need' he said 'I rather think that I have had a visit from Mr Mischief.'
    He was right!
    Outside Mr Happy's house, and running away as fast as his little legs would carry
    him, was a small mischievous figure.
    Mr Mischief!

    [Roger Hargreaves, *Mr Mischief*, Thurman Publishing, 1978]

4.3 Instrument–purpose patterns

In the last section, you saw that Mr Skinny went to live with Mr Greedy in order to put on weight. When we use a phrase such as *in order to*, we use it to show that there is a reason or a purpose for an action or activity. We can put this into a table as follows:

Instrument	Purpose
Mr Skinny goes to live with Mr Greedy.	Mr Skinny wants to put on weight.

With the Mr Skinny story we can see that Mr Skinny actually does put on weight. So he achieves his purpose. We can put that into this table:

Instrument	Achievement
Mr Skinny goes to live with Mr Greedy.	Mr Skinny does put on weight.

You can see that the ideas of 'purpose' and 'achievement' are very close. You have a purpose when you want to achieve something; your purpose is your 'hoped-for' achievement.

ACTIVITY 41

What is the 'instrument' and what are the purpose and the achievement in this extract?

> *'So you see' said Mr Bounce finally 'You must give me something to stop me bouncing about all over the place quite so much.'*
> *'Hmmm' pondered the doctor.*
> *After some thought Dr Makeyouwell went to his medicine cabinet and took out a pair of tiny red boots.*
> *'This should do the trick' he told Mr Bounce*
> *'Heavy boots! That should stop the bouncing!'*
> *'Oh thank you Dr Makeyouwell' said Mr Bounce and walked home wearing his red boots.*
> *Not bounced!*
> *Walked!*

[Roger Hargreaves, *Mr Bounce*, Thurman Publishing, 1976]

4.4 Problem–solution patterns

If we look back over some of the texts that we have studied in this chapter, we can see that in a number of them there have been problems that have needed and sometimes gained solutions:

● *Mr Skinny was extraordinarily thin.* – Mr Skinny needed to put on weight. He went to stay with Mr Greedy. Mr Skinny then put on weight – or at least he gained a tummy. Mr Skinny was very happy.

- *Mr Bounce was very small and like a rubber ball.* – Mr Bounce bounced all over the place. He went to the Doctor. The Doctor gave him some heavy boots. Mr Bounce stopped bouncing.

We can organise these outlines into four parts:

Situation	*Mr Skinny was extraordinarily thin.*	*Mr Bounce was very small and like a rubber ball.*
Problem	Mr Skinny needed to put on weight.	Mr Bounce bounced all over the place.
Solution	He went to stay with Mr Greedy. Mr Skinny then put on weight – or at least he gained a tummy.	He went to the doctor. The doctor gave him some heavy boots
Evaluation	Mr Skinny was very happy.	Mr Bounce stopped bouncing.

- **Situation**, or background: Where are we? Who is involved? When is this happening? What things or circumstances create the 'problem' in the next part?
- **Problem**: What difficulty, need, complication, doubt, and so on, emerges from the situation?
- **Solution**: How was the difficulty, complication or doubt resolved, the need met, the harm avoided, and so on?
- **Evaluation**: Was the solution a good one? Is there more than one solution? Which is the best one?

These particular parts of the pattern can be signalled for the reader by certain words or phrases used in the text itself.

If you look back to the text about Mr Bounce, you can see that there are certain phrases in the text that suggest that there is a problem. For instance, Mr Bounce says *You must give me something to stop me bouncing about all over the place quite so much*. Mr Bounce wants his bouncing *stopped*. Doctor Makeyouwell gives him the heavy boots and says *This should do the trick*. These words suggest that Doctor Makeyouwell has the solution to Mr Bounce's problem.

Now read this advertisement from an advertising brochure that is commonly found in British homes. As you read the advertisement, decide what the problem is that the items offered for sale are trying to solve.

> *If you wear glasses, combatting bright sunlight has always meant one of two solutions – either irritating clip-ons or costly prescription sunglasses. Now there's a third option in the shape of these wrap-arounds. These smart sunglasses are designed to be worn over regular corrective specs, preventing the ingress of harsh sunlight from any angle and eliminating 100% of the sun's harmful rays.*
> ***Wrap-Around Sunglasses £8.95***
>
> [Innovations (Mail Order) plc, May–September 1996]

As with the Mr Bounce text, certain words or phrases signal the various parts of the pattern. The **situation** involves those who wear glasses; the **problem** is *combatting bright sunlight* if you wear glasses. The text then suggests two **solutions** to that problem: *irritating clip-ons* or *costly prescription sunglasses*. However, you can see that the words *irritating* and *costly* suggest a negative

evaluation. This returns you to the original **problem**, for which the company has come up with a **solution**: *the shape of these wrap-arounds*. There is then a positive **evaluation** of the **solution**: *preventing the ingress* and *eliminating 100% of the sun's harmful rays*. We can set this out in a grid as follows:

Situation	*you wear glasses*	*you wear glasses*
Problem	*combatting bright sunlight*	*combatting bright sunlight*
Solution	**1** *clip-ons* **2** *prescription sunglasses*	*the shape of these wrap-arounds*
Evaluation	(Negative) **1** *irritating [clip-ons]* **2** *costly [prescription sunglasses]* Return to original problem	(Positive) **1** *preventing the ingress of harsh sunlight from any angle* **2** *eliminating 100% of the sun's harmful rays*

You can see from this grid that problem–solution patterns can be recurrent within a particular text.

ACTIVITY 42

1 Now look at the following text, and construct your own grid:

Mahogany-effect video library

The cost of pre-recorded videos is coming down rapidly, which means our collections of favourite films and programmes are growing equally fast. The trouble is boxed videos are not the most attractive things to keep on open display, which makes this handsome piece of furniture all the more invaluable. Finished in a realistic mahogany-effect, our cabinet stores no less than 48 boxed videos (or an even greater number of books if desired) on six shelves, accessible from both sides – yet it looks good enough for the most sophisticated or traditional living room environment. 76 cm (30") high, it requires just 31 H 30 cm (12 1/4" × 11 3/4") of floor space and smoothly revolves on a swivelling base to give optimum access to the shelves.

[Innovations (Mail Order) plc, May–September 1997]

2 Sometimes the problem is not stated at the beginning of the text but occurs after the **evaluation** that tells you how wonderful the product is. Look at this part of an advertisement, from the same brochure as the previous two. After you have read it, create a table for this example, as you have done for the previous text.

The Wizard Pillow

The Wizard Pillow's nodular surface massages and relaxes the head and neck during sleep, providing even, well-ventilated support. The specially designed neck roll correctly aligns the upper spine, helping relieve stresses and relax the muscles in the neck and shoulders to help give a perfect night's sleep.

[Innovations (Mail Order) plc, May–September 1996]

The relationship between the **situation** and the **problem** may also be a cause–consequence pattern. We can see this in mahogany-effect video library text, if we set it out in the following form:

Cause	Consequence
The cost of pre-recorded videos is coming down rapidly…	*… our collections of favourite films and programmes are growing equally fast*

These patterns are further signalled in the text by the phrase *which means*, which could be replaced by either *causing* or *causes*.

In addition, the relationship between **solution** and **evaluation** can also make up an **instrument–achievement** pattern. In this text, the pattern is as follows:

Instrument	Achievement
[it] revolves on a swivelling base	*optimum access to the shelves*

Here the signalling is absolutely explicit in the phrase *to give*, which could be expanded to read *in order to give*.

We have here examples in which patterns are **combined**, **multilayered** or **embedded** one within another.

ACTIVITY 43

Look at this text from the *Independent on Sunday*. As you read the text, answer these questions:

1 What was the original situation?

2 What was the problem?

3 There are two possible solutions to that problem. What are they?

> *US Court lets Tribe Set Punishment*
>
> **Young Alaskan offenders face island exile**
>
> *from Phil Reeves*
> *in Los Angeles*
>
> [1] *Let the Home Secretary huff and puff about the importance of being tough on young criminals. He's still as soft as the driven snow compared with the Tlingit Indians of Alaska. Their solution? Banishment to a remote island.*
>
> [2] *Tribal elders in a fishing village in south-east Alaska are to decide this week whether to dispatch two 17-year-old boys to separate uninhabited islands for a year, equipped only with a limited amount of food and tools as a punishment for a violent robbery.*
>
> [3] *In the first case of its kind in the United States, the youths, both Tlingits, have been handed over to their tribe by and American judge who was reluctant to jail them under compulsory sentencing laws.*
>
> [4] *The two, Simon Roberts and Adrian Guthrie, have admitted stealing $40 [£25] from a pizza deliveryman and hitting him over the head with a baseball bat, during a visit to the state of Washington last year. Roberts (who wielded the bat) faces up to five-and-a-half years in jail, while Guthrie could be sentenced to a maximum of 41 months. Instead, James Allendoerfer, a Superior Court judge in Washington's Snohomish County, agreed to allow them to return to their remote home village of*

Klawock, on Prince of Wales Island, where a council of elders, dressed in tribal regalia, will convene to decide their fate on Tuesday.

[5] *Last week the pair were released from county jail into the custody of two Tlingit guards who had come to escort them on the 800 mile journey back to their fishing community.*

[6] *Before releasing them, Judge Allendoerfer conducted an investigation into the conditions the boys would face during their island sojourn, and the degree to which they would be supervised. They have been ordered to return to his court for sentencing in 18 months, when they may escape jail terms if he feels their banishment has done them any good.*

[7] *Bill Jaquette, Guthrie's lawyer, believes the tribe does not have many choices other than to banish the boys. "Most of the other traditional punishments are pretty radical, like chopping off limbs, and staking people to the beach at low tide. Of course, there is the option of shunning them … But their crime is too serious for that."*

[8] *… The boys are expected to receive some survival training. They will have a limited number of tools – "bows, arrows, knives, but no guns," said Jaquette, – and enough food to last two weeks. Their likely destination will be one of the thousands of small, heavily forested islands of south-east Alaska, populated by bear and deer.*

[9] *After their supplies are exhausted, they will have to fend for themselves, fishing, hunting, and clam-digging. Although the climate is mild compared with Alaska's Arctic reaches, the winters are snowy and punctuated by fierce storms. And there are up to 200 inches of rain a year in some areas.*

[10] *The judge's decision followed intense lobbying by an Indian tribal judge, Rudy James, who … has said banishment is mandatory under Indian traditional law for an offence of such severity, and would compel the boys to atone for their crimes and cleanse their spirits. The boys would be visited at regular intervals. "We won't let them die," he said.*

[11] *Meanwhile the tribe is planning to compensate the deliveryman, who suffered permanent vision and hearing damage, with a $150,000 house and medical expenses, "In our society no individual stands by themselves," Mr. James said, "In glory the whole tribe is with them. And also in shame."*

[12] *The boys have said they would be happier to be banished to an island than locked up. They believe they have the necessary survival skills, having been brought up … in a fishing and logging village where most people know how to fish and hunt, "We have been raised our whole lives living off the land, knowing what to eat and what not to eat," Roberts said, "I feel confident I can survive."*

[13] *In 1979, Frank Brown, a Bella Bella Kwakiutl Indian, was handed over to tribal elders after a court in Canada convicted him of robbery. After spending eight months on a island, Brown returned to go to college, and went on to become a much-admired canoe-maker.*

[adapted from the *Independent on Sunday*, August 1994]

Now that you have read the passage, answer the following questions:

1 What are the problems and the solutions in each of paragraphs 1, 3 and 11?

2 What are the causes and consequences in paragraphs 4 and 10? If that seems a difficult question to answer, then answer these questions: (a) In paragraph 4, what would be usual consequence of these questions? (b) In paragraph 10, what does Rudy James think would be the result of the boys' banishment?

3 What opinions or 'evaluations' are being made or given in paragraphs 3, 7 and 12?

WRITING ACTIVITY P

Look at some of the letters and their replies in an 'agony column' in a magazine or newspaper. Analyse them for the **situation–problem–solution–evaluation** pattern. What kinds of evaluations of solutions are given in these kinds of texts? Using your analysis as a model, write your own letters and replies.

4.5 Predictive patterns

In Chapter 3, we looked at text nouns. You saw that these kinds of words refer to other pieces of the text; they appear to gather up information in the text and summarise it. You came across words such as *situation, fact, move, problem*, and so on.

However, not only can these words be used to refer back to parts of a text but, as we have seen, they can also be used to predict what will happen next in the text. Let's look at a text that you have seen before – but this time the text is stopped after the third sentence:

> *As anyone with a younger brother or sister will know, most families now use disposable nappies. They make the whole business much easier. But there are four big problems with them.*

▷ What question do you automatically ask here?

The rest of the text answers that question:

> *First, trees have to be cut down and turned to pulp which makes the soft inside of each nappy. Second, to make the nappy look white, the pulp is bleached, possibly with chlorine which pollutes rivers. Third, a lot of each nappy is plastic, which is difficult to dispose of. Finally, used nappies take up a lot of space in landfill sites.*
>
> [Lewis Bronze, Nick Heathcote and Peter Brown, *The Blue Peter Green Book*, BBC Books/Sainsbury's, 1990]

You can see that if we stop the text at the sentence at which we have stopped it, the emphasis tends to lie on the number *four*. And in the text that follows you are given the four problems indicated by the words *First, second, third* and *finally*.

ACTIVITY 44

Now look at the following text from Charles Dickens' *The Old Curiosity Shop*, which you will have already seen above. How does this follow a predictive pattern?

Now, the ladies being together under these circumstances, it was extremely natural that the discourse should turn upon the propensity of mankind to tyrannise over the weaker sex, and the duty that devolved upon the weaker sex to resist that tyranny and assert their rights and dignity. It was natural for four reasons: firstly, because Mrs. Quilp being a young woman and notoriously under the dominion of her husband ought to be excited to rebel; secondly, because Mrs. Quilp's parent was known to be laudably shrewish in her dispostion and inclined to resist male authority; thirdly, because each visitor wished to show for herself how superior she was in this respect to the generality of her sex; and fourthly, because the company being accustomed to scandalise each other in pairs, were deprived of their usual subject of conversation now that they were all assembled in close friendship, and had consequently no better employment than to attack the common enemy.

[Charles Dickens, *The Old Curiosity Shop*]

Not all predictive patterns in this form use an exact number.

ACTIVITY 45

1 Read this passage, and as you do so decide what kind of text it comes from:

Recently, we have introduced a number of new developments. Our payment outlets network has been increased to over 19,000 nationwide. Area office opening hours have been extended and new direct telephone numbers are now available which put you through directly to the person you need. And to save you money, we have introduced reductions if you pay your bill promptly or by monthly direct debit.

Which word in the text **predicts** what follows? What phrase is used here instead of the exact number that you had in the Dickens extract? What are the exact number of new developments?

2 In the following text, the **predictive patterning** comes in two parts. What are the words that **predict**? What are the things that they predict? How are the forms of the two **predictive** elements similar? When you work on the answer to that last question, think of the grammar.

To give your pregnancy the best possible start, it's a good idea to think ahead. There are a number of steps you can take, which will not only increase your chances of conception, but will be your best guarantee of having a normal, healthy baby. Ideally, you and your partner should plan for pregnancy at least three months before you conceive. It is in the first few weeks, when you may not even know you are pregnant, that the baby's development can be most easily affected. So, keeping fit and eating well will ensure you have done as much as you can to nourish and protect the baby in the womb. There may be other things to consider too; perhaps there are hazards at work, which could affect the baby's health, or maybe you missed being vaccinated against German measles at school. Planning for pregnancy gives you the time you need to consider these kinds of risks and, if necessary, to do something positive about them.

[Elizabeth Fenwick, *The Complete Johnson and Johnson Book of Mother and Baby Care*, Dorling Kindersley, 1990]

Another good **predictive** device is the question. Read through the following passage.

▷ Where is the question answered?

Seventy million years ago, in a place now know as the Hell Creek Formation, in Montana, a Tyrannosaurus rex *stood over the gouged-out carcass of a* Triceratops, *gnawing on its hip-bone. Was it murder? Or did* T. rex *simply stumble across the* Triceratops *corpse and feast on the carrion?*

Nobody knows. Palaeontologists have been divided for nearly a century over whether T. rex *was primarily a predator or a scavenger. A definitive verdict would influence theories of dinosaur ecology. It could also ruin* T. rex's *reputation: to lump it with other scavengers such as the unloved vulture would spoil* T. rex's *burgeoning Hollywood career.*

Proponents of the scavenging T. rex *have plenty of circumstantial evidence, mainly in the dinosaur's build: small eyes (poor for hunting), small arms (poor for grabbing), and thick hind legs (poor for sprinting), for example. Some have also suggested that its famously long teeth would snap during the thrashing and bone-crushing of predation. But this notion, at least, can now be tossed out. In a study in the week's* Nature, *Gregory Erickson, a doctoral student at the University of California, Berkeley, and colleagues at Stanford University show that the teeth and jaws of* T. rex *were easily sturdy enough to withstand the rigours of a live kill.*

[*The Economist*, 24 August 1996]

Another way of predicting is through the use of punctuation, particularly with colons.

ACTIVITY 46

These next two extracts both use colons to introduce text that follows. They are both taken from an article, in a magazine for English teachers, that summarises changes to A- and AS-level English examinations. Read the two extracts.

As you read them, consider the following. What are the different functions of the two extracts? What are the differences between the organisation of the two extracts? What is the relationship between the two functions of the extracts and the two different forms of organisation of the text?

1   *The Cores are all written to the same format:*

1. *Aims. These are additions to the 1997 Cores, which attempt to define the specific aims of the separate English courses. All three Cores refer to developing skills in speech, reading and writing.*

2. *Principles for Syllabus Construction. These are identical for all subjects, and included continuity and progression from GCSE; development of skills in communication, application of number and IT; identification of opportunities for students to improve their own learning and performance, work with others and solve problems; indication of ways in which the subject can contribute to an understanding of spiritual, moral and cultural issues. [etc.]*

2   *The Aims of AS/A English Literature courses are familiar in their references to: interest and enjoyment, reading widely and critically, developing confident, independent readers, expressing responses effectively through speech and writing,*

reflecting on own responses to texts and considering other readers' interpretations. The significant additions, especially for readers skilled in reading subtexts, are these:

- *A/AS course should involve an introduction to the great traditions of English literature.*

- *AS students should use critical concepts and terminology with understanding and discrimination.*

- *A2 students should be encouraged to use detailed knowledge of individual texts to explore comparisons and connections … and to appreciate the significance of cultural and historical influences upon readers and writers.*

[*The English & Media Magazine*, no. 36, Summer 1997]

WRITING ACTIVITY Q

Look at the above two extracts again. They were written for a readership, or audience, of teachers and lecturers in English. The writing is formal and often quite dense. Think about the courses that you are studying at the moment.

1 Write a formal summary of the course, giving the detailed aims, requirements and syllabus.

2 Write a brochure to attract potential students to study the course. Use different predictive devices, such as the question–answer pattern. Make sure that your writing is informal enough to appeal to people of around your own age or younger. What other predictive patterns can you set up and use in this kind of brochure?

3 When you have finished the writing, ask yourselves what the relationship is between these devices and the level of formality of any piece of writing.

4.6 Sets of expectations

There are very few occasions on which we read something without having a reason for reading it. Most of us pick up a newspaper and scan through the headlines to see which articles are likely to interest us. We are unlikely to pick up a book without knowing the author, or being interested by the title, or the subject matter. We often read books because of the reviews we have read or the recommendations of a friend. Increasingly, we read books because we have seen the film. In each of these cases, we read because we have some expectations of what we will find when we turn to the first page. This section examines the ways in which those expectations are set up.

▷ What is happening here?

Sally first tried letting loose a team of gophers. The plan backfired when a dog chased them away. She then entertained a group of teenagers and was delighted when they brought their motorcycles. Unfortunately, she failed to find a Peeping Tom listed in the Yellow Pages. Furthermore, her stereosystem was not loud enough. The crab grass might have worked but she didn't have a fan that was sufficiently powerful. The obscene phone calls gave her hope until the number was changed. She thought about calling a door-to-door salesman but decided to hang up a clothes-line instead. It was

*the installation of blinking neon lights across the street that did the trick. She
eventually framed an ad from the classified section.*

[J. D. Bransford, B. S. Stein and T. Shelton, 'Learning from the perspective of the
comprehender', in J. C. Alderson and A. H. Urquhart (eds), *Reading in a Foreign
Language*, Longman, 1984]

Turn the book over and try to recall the passage: the best way is to try to tell the
story to the person sitting next to you.

▷ How easy is it to remember and recall?
▷ What do you think *crab grass* is?

A suggested title is 'Attempts to get her neighbours to move'.

▷ How easy is the passage to recall now?
▷ What do you think *crab grass* is, now that you know the title?

Now look at the following text.

▷ What *two* interpretations could there be of this?

> *Every Saturday night, four good friends get together. When Jerry, Mike, and Pat
> arrived, Karen was sitting in her living room writing some notes. She quickly
> gathered the cards and stood up to greet her friends at the door. They followed her into
> the living room but as usual they couldn't agree on exactly what to play. Jerry
> eventually took the stand and set things up. Finally, they began to play. Karen's
> recorder filled the room with soft and pleasant music. Early in the evening, Mike
> noticed Pat's hand and the many diamonds …*

[Anderson *et al.* (1977), cited in G. Brown and G. Yule, *Discourse Analysis*,
Cambridge University Press, 1983]

This text was given firstly to a group of female students who were planning a
career as music teachers; it was given next to a group of male students from a
weight-lifting class.

▷ What interpretations do you think they came up with for the text?

These texts show that it is often the expectations that we bring to a text that
allow us to make sense of it. Where do we get these expectations from? As you
can see from the previous example, it may be our background that allows us to
make sense of a text, that allows us to interpret it.

This is often true of advertising. In the left-hand column below are a group of
slogans from advertisements. Match them with the companies on the right-hand
side:

1 **Miami** from £278 return	**a** Direct Line Insurance
2 If you knew how much you're being overcharged for life cover the shock could kill you.	**b** Anthisan Plus Sting Relief Spray.
3 Nobody congratulated me on my promotion more sincerely, affectionately, generously and thrillingly, than I did myself.	**c** Waitrose

4 Flying Doctor.   **d** Toyota

5 All the better for you.   **e** De Beers Diamond Mines.

6 See it want it win it.   **f** Virgin MegaSavers.

See page 82 for the answers.

In the above passage, you have looked at the way in which we can build up expectations of **things** that we read about. We also have expectations about the order in which we will find things. We can see this if we think about visits to the dentist. When we visit the dentist, we have expectations of the 'things' that we will find there: a set of drills; a receptionist's desk; a dentist's chair; a radio playing Radio 2; a receptionist; a dentist, often in a white coat; a waiting room; upright and/or comfortable chairs; a display case with toothbrushes, toothpaste and so on; a computer with patients' records; a white porcelain bowl and a supply of running water so that you can rinse your mouth.

Now look through this list again.

▷ Are these things from the dentist's in the right order?
▷ What does 'the right order' mean?
▷ Where do we get 'the right order' from?

Now put the things in the right order.

How would you feel if the 'dentist' arrived wearing a lumberjack's shirt, a hard hat and heavy boots, and wielding a chainsaw?

We have expectations of the **things** that we will find in certain situations. We also have expectations of the **order** we will find them in. This is true in our reading too.

ACTIVITY 47

1 In the European tradition of fairy tales, there are some 'common elements': a beautiful princess; a handsome prince; a wicked stepmother with long black hair who may or may not be a witch; if no stepmother then a witch – with long black hair; a rather ineffectual father; lots of talking animals… now think about adding some more. Then think about the order in which these things 'traditionally' come. Does the handsome prince rescue the princess at the beginning of the story? Now read the following 'feminist fable' by Suniti Namjoshi.

How does it differ from the 'traditional fairy tale' that you have just thought about? In what sense is it a 'feminist' fairy tale?

THE OYSTER CHILD

Once upon a time there was an oyster child. She never said a word, didn't give a damn, just lived quietly at the bottom of the ocean, and did what she could, which in effect meant doing nothing and keeping very still, to protect herself. This required constant effort and she developed an ulcer; but she kept on at it, protecting herself from within herself and keeping her mouth shut tight. Then one day a diver found her and cut her open. Inside the oyster was the most beautiful pearl anyone had seen. Its near perfection, its extraordinary size, its gentle lustre were absolutely amazing. Everyone came from far and near solely to admire it.

And was the oyster pleased? She was probably pleased, but for obvious reasons she said nothing.

Question: Why did the oyster say nothing?
a. From habit.
b. Because by this time she was already dead.
c. Out of sheer modesty.

[Suniti Namjoshi, *Feminist Fables*, Virago, 1994]

2   Think very carefully about the purpose of titles. What is the purpose of headlines in newspapers? What is the purpose of the titles of books? List some book titles and think about their purpose, how closely they are related to the content of the book, and how much the age of the reader is related to the clarity, or otherwise, of the title of a book.

WRITING ACTIVITY R

All families have stories. Ask your parents, or your relatives, to tell you a story that they remember well about your family. Listen carefully to the story. Take time to think about it carefully. Picture for yourself the situation in which it happened. Imagine the details of the situation: what the weather was like, what the people were wearing, what time of day it was, and what the buildings or countryside were like in which the story is set. Write the story down yourself. Then take the story back to the person who first told it to you.

What differences does your original informant find between your version of the story and the one that he or she has in his or her head? Why do you think that these differences are there?

Answers to exercise on expectations in Section 4.6

1, f (Virgin); 2, a (Direct Line); 3, e (De Beers); 4, b (Anthisan); 5, c (Waitrose); 6, d (Toyota).

5 Looking at conversation

5.0 Introduction

So far, we have looked at written texts. In this final chapter, you will be looking at some more written texts; this time, however, they will be the written transcripts of speech.

Before we go any further, write down all of the differences that you feel there are between speech and writing.

You may have come up with lists that include some of the following points. You may wish to agree or disagree with any or all of what follows:

Written text

1 It is 'grammatically correct'.

2 It is written with punctuation into sentences.

3 It is permanent and can be read again and again.

4 It is 'context free'. The writer sits down with a blank piece of paper or a clear computer screen.

5 It is carefully considered and doesn't have to respond immediately to a situation.

6 It is not interfered with as it is written.

Speech

1 It is often grammatically 'incorrect'.

2 There is no punctuation and it is not in sentences.

3 It is impermanent. You can't hear it again and again. You certainly can't ask the speaker to repeat it time and time again.

4 It is created as a response to the situation and context of the speakers.

5 It is spontaneous.

6 It takes place under conditions that are full of other interference: for example, the noise of the 8.15 to Winchester passing the window; spoken while the last resident at the bar demands a last order from the long- suffering barman; as the dog is tugging on the lead; and so on.

There are many other differences between written and spoken discourse. Your list may well be quite different to the above version.

It may be thought, because of what you have looked at in the book so far, that spoken discourse is far less likely to be cohesive and coherent than written discourse. However, spoken discourse *is* coherent. If it wasn't coherent, we simply couldn't have conversations. But its coherence is rather mysterious. As two recent writers on the subject have put it,

> *… most of the descriptive problems in the analysis of spoken discourse remain to be solved.*

> [M. Coulthard and D. Brazil, in M. Coulthard (ed.), *Advances in Spoken Discourse Analysis*, Routledge, 1992]

Note the rather academic **register**.

What is clear, however, is that people will always try to understand what someone is saying, however bizarre that utterance sounds. And in looking at spoken discourse, you must ask yourself the question which you ask naturally every time you hear somebody speak: 'Why are they saying that?' When you are in a conversation with someone, you ask that question and answer it at the same time, but subconsciously. And as you answer the question, so you work out and say your reply. But there seem to be a number of rules that affect what we can say in reply.

5.1 How to do things with words: the functions of speech

Imagine that a murder trial is taking place in your town. You go to the court house. Somehow, you slip past the policeman at the door of the court room. You run into the court and shout to the defendant: *I sentence you to death!* What would happen to you next?

Yes, the policeman who should have stopped you in the first place would probably grab you by the neck. The judge would probably tell you that you were in contempt of court. And you would find yourself facing either a fine, or imprisonment, or both. But why?

Essentially, the problem is that you had taken the judge's words from him. It is not your place, literally, to say those words. You are not the right person, the judge, in the right place, the court, at the right time, at the end of the trial, the sentencing. You might have been saying them to the correct person, but you don't have the *right* to say those words.

There are certain phrases which, when said, actually perform a **<u>function</u>**.

ACTIVITY 48

What does the Queen say as the bottle of champagne smashes on the front of a boat that is being launched? What does the priest or the registrar say when the bride and the groom have finished saying their vows? What would happen if *you* said those words?

There are, then, a small group of set phrases which, when spoken by the right person, in the right place, at the right time and also to the right people, actually do the things that they say. In fact, it would be possible even for the right people to violate those terms. If the Queen smashed a bottle of champagne over a radio-controlled model boat, on the lake in the grounds of Buckingham Palace, and said *I name this ship the Britannia*, this would be seen as a joke on her part. If the vicar said *I pronounce you man and wife* to a great dane and a dachshund, at the end of the vicarage tea party, then someone might send for a breathalyser.

But we all do certain things with words. We use things called **performative verbs**; such as *dare, promise, bet, warn, challenge*. We say things such as:

> *I challenge you to a race round the restaurant. Winner buys the meal.*
> *I bet you a fiver Mavis leaves the Street before the end of the year.*
> *I promise you I'll get you all the money in the world.*
> *I dare you to go up to him and tell him he's got a bald patch.*

We can informally test whether or not a verb is performative by putting *I hereby* at the beginning of the sentence. In general, if the sentence then does not sound possible, the verb is not performative.

ACTIVITY 49

Test these sentences for performative verbs:

> *I dare you to rob that bank.*
> *I have got two lovely coconuts.*
> *I warn you that Gromit will bite.*
> *I bequeath you my house and all its contents.*
> *I think that I will watch the television.*
> *I believe that the moon is made of Wensleydale cheese.*
> *I state that I am of sound mind.*
> *I nominate Paul Andrews as Chairman of the Students' Council.*
> *I catch the bus to college every day.*
> *I order you to leave me some of your chips.*

It is perhaps worth repeating that what is important here is that these words are actually **doing** things as they are spoken. They are known as **speech acts**.

However, you can see that each of the above sentences begins with *I*. In the real world, we do things with words all the time. If I go into the chip shop and say *Can I have a bag of chips and a pickled egg, please?*, what am I doing? There are a number of labels that we can put on what I have just done, but we might want to say that I am 'politely requesting'. This is important because that is what we understand the words to **mean**. If I went into the chip shop, made my polite request, and the people behind the counter simply said *Yes* and then stood there with their hands on their hips, we would not be amused. We would not have wanted them to think that I was asking about my ability to buy a bag of chips, or even the possibility of buying a bag of chips. In this case – and in much else that we do with conversation – our utterances perform **functions**.

ACTIVITY 50

1 Look through the following spoken items. What is each of them doing? In other words, what is the function of each sentence?

> *I'm going to the pictures with some mates tonight. Do you want to join us?*
> *If you could lend me a tenner, I'd be really grateful*
> *If I could just come in here.*
> *I'm thinking of ringing Tariq Latif about it.*
> *Shall I collect the drinks for you?*
> *Would it be at all possible for me to borrow your Porsche?*
> *Yes, well I see what you mean, but I think there is another view here.*
> *I'm sorry but I wasn't sure what you meant by saying that we could all join in.*
> *I'm not quite sure how to put this but I'm afraid your cat is going to have to be put down.*
> *I was wondering if it might be OK to skip the session tomorrow.*

A list of suggested functions follows. Which ones did you have? Did you have different names for the same functions?

Apologising	Inviting
Asking for clarification	Offering
Asking permission	Requesting
Interrupting	Requesting
Interrupting	Stating an intention

Note the grammatical form of each of the suggestions.

2 Think of at least four other ways of saying any of the functions in the above list. For example, think of four other ways of offering. Think of the most polite way to offer. Then think of the rudest way to offer. Finally, think of at least two other ways of offering. Put all of your suggestions into order, ranging from the most polite to the least polite.

Look at the differences in form of the different ways of saying any of the functions. These different forms for each function are often called the **exponents** of each function.

With which people could you use the different forms? What are the differences between these people? In answering this question, you should consider their emotional distance from you and also their power relationship with you. For example, which exponents of the function would you use with the college principal? Which exponents would you use with your friends? Remember that your friends usually have a more equal power relationship with you.

5.2 Co-operating in the conversation

Our account of an unsuccessful visit to the chip shop does suggest, however, that we can only do things successfully if the other people involved in the conversation are willing to co-operate. It would be no good if the vicar were to pronounce a couple man and wife if they didn't want him to do it. That would violate one of the necessary conditions for the vicar to pronounce them man and wife. It would be no good daring your best friend to ask one of the college lecturers out for a meal, if your friend didn't want to accept the dare, or to listen to what you had to say. Conversation only works when the people engaged in it co-operate with each other. But co-operation can be a very elusive thing to pin down.

Look at the following example of 'written conversation' from Carson McCullers' novella, *The Ballad of the Sad Café*.

▷ What is the author suggesting about the relationship of the two people in the story by their conversation at this point? Think particularly about Cousin Lymon's interruption.

> *[Miss Amelia's] father was also an interminable subject which was dear to her.*
> *'Why, Law,' she would say to Lymon. 'Those days I slept. I'd go to bed just as the lamp was turned on and sleep – why, I'd sleep like I was drowned in warm axle grease. Then come daybreak Big Papa would walk in and put his hand down on my shoulder. "Get stirring, Little," he would say. "White meat and gravy. Ham and eggs." And I'd run down the stairs and dress by the hot stove while he was out washing at the pump. Then off we'd go to the still or maybe – '*
> *'The grits we had this morning was poor,' Cousin Lymon said. 'Fried too quick so that the inside never heated.'*
> *'And when Big Papa would run off the liquor in those days –' The conversation would go on endlessly, with Miss Amelia's long legs stretched out before the hearth; …*
> [Carson McCullers, *The Ballad of the Sad Café*, Penguin, 1963]

As was said above, one person will go out of his or her way to make one utterance relevant to another person. In this way, they apply the **co-operative principle**. The American linguistic philosopher H. Paul Grice first suggested the co-operative principle in 1967. He suggested that people co-operate in conversation in four particular ways, which he formulated as the following **maxims**:

1   Maxim of Quality – Tell the truth.
2   Maxim of Quantity – Don't say too much, and don't say too little.
3   Maxim of Manner – Don't be obscure, ambiguous or ramble on.
4   Maxim of Relevance – Be relevant.

As we have seen from the brief dialogue above, it is always possible to break any and all of these maxims. In fact, people break – or flout – the maxims all the time. When they do this they imply certain things. Grice called this **'conversational implicature'**.

If one girl said to another

> *Does your boyfriend often catch the bus to Rochdale?*

and if the first girl knew that the boy lived in the opposite direction from Rochdale, would she simply be asking for information? Would she want the first girl simply to answer *No* and forget about it? Which maxim would the first girl have broken? To help you answer that, think of the reply that the second girl would make.

However, not all conversation is of this rather 'nudge–nudge, wink–wink' nature. In fact, this is quite an easy example of implicature because it flouts the

maxims quite openly. Implicature is often more commonplace and more subtle.
Take this, for example:

> *A. Are you going past the pub on the way home?*
> *B. I've got to collect the dog from the vets.*

▷ What kind of reply does A want?
▷ What is – saying to A here?
▷ Which of the maxims does B's reply flout?
▷ Which of the other maxims makes B's reply understandable?

ACTIVITY 51
Look at these groups of utterances and responses. What is actually being said?
For each pair consider which maxim, or maxims, is flouted.

1 *A: I've run out of petrol.*
   B: There's a garage round the corner.

2 *A: Is Mavis in this morning?*
   B: There's a red Vauxhall outside her gate.

3 *A: Does Mavis have a boyfriend?*
   B: There's a red Vauxhall outside her gate.

4 *A: I didn't know Mavis drove.*
   B: Oh, that'll be the brother visiting from Singapore.

5 *A: Does Mavis still own the corner shop?*
   B: Died last year.

6 *A: Can I open the window?*
   B: I didn't know you didn't like smoking.

5.3 Being polite

We have just looked at the way in which people can co-operate in a conversation.
If people follow all of the maxims, the conversation can be very efficient. Things
will be said quickly, relevantly, truthfully and clearly. But a quick glance at that
list will show that all of those things are not enough. If the boss said to the
secretary

> *Type this letter.*

he or she would be all of those things – quick, relevant, truthful and clear. But he
or she wouldn't be polite. Being polite is often central to why people break Grice's
maxims. In fact, Grice himself thought that a full account of co-operation in
conversation would have to pay attention to being polite.

So the boss needs to think a little bit about how to deal with the secretary. There
is a trade-off between being efficient and being polite.

Being polite is seen as being two things. The first is the need to be part of the crowd, to be accepted by your group. This group can be found anywhere: at school, at college, at work, in your family or at the pub. We all want to be part of the group. We want to be accepted. Because of this need to be accepted, we usually try to be **tactful**. Being tactful again means two things. First, you have to try to avoid demanding things from the other person. Second, you have to try to offer something to the other person. Take this example:

> *Mummy Bear: Somebody's eaten my porridge.*
> *Goldilocks: Well, it wasn't me.*

Mummy Bear has not said *Goldilocks has eaten my porridge*. If she had done that she would have demanded that Goldilocks either own up or defend herself. Also, because Mummy Bear has said **Somebody***'s eaten my porridge*, she has not suggested that Goldilocks has done the dastardly deed. So Mummy Bear has offered Goldilocks a way out, which Goldilocks has taken.

The other part of politeness is being **respectful**. Now, think about this carefully. What happens to you when you are respectful? If you are respectful, you may avoid others placing demands on you. When there are fewer demands on you, you remain independent, and because of that you have more freedom.

Thus politeness involves placing fewer demands on others, and avoiding demands on yourself. This is shown in language by the use of phrases such as *just, a bit of, only,* and so on, as in:

> *I just need to know the time of the train.*
> *It is a bit more expensive.*
> *It only needs a minute of your time.*

These phrases help to lessen the impact of the statement or demand. Alternatively, you could rather slyly offer people a choice:

> *If you've got the time, could you run off those copies, please.*
> *Would you mind shutting the door, please?*
> *Could you let me borrow your computer for ten minutes?*

Another version is to appear to be pessimistic. You pretend that the hearer is unwilling or unable to help. This is often done by using negatives and tag questions:

> *You couldn't lend me your computer for ten minutes, could you?*
> *You wouldn't mind shutting the door, would you?*

Another strategy is called 'hedging' and involves using phrases such as *sort of, I suppose, by any chance*:

> *You wouldn't happen to have a quid, I suppose?*

As you can see, it is possible to combine any number of these strategies.

▷ How do these strategies relate to the functions that we discussed in Section 5.1?

Another way is to appear jokey. This helps to emphasise that both you and the hearer are part of the group. It is being **tactful** by a different route altogether:

> *So who's asked Julie out on Friday, then, nudge, nudge, wink, wink, say no more!*
> *I hear somebody smashed up Daddy's wheels at the weekend!*

The other way of avoiding demands is by thinking what the benefits and costs are to your hearers. If you are offering them a cup of coffee, then the benefits are high and the costs are low. You will not need to be so polite. If you are asking them to give you a lift somewhere, then the benefits to them are likely to be few, and the costs high. In that case you will need to be very polite.

> *Coffee, John?*
> *You couldn't give me a lift to the party tonight, could you?*

or even

> *I was wondering if you'd mind giving me a lift to the party tonight.*

The opposite to politeness is generally thought to be rudeness. In what way are people rude? People are often rude by being verbally threatening. They can be 'in your face'. This idea of 'face' is often very important when it comes to politeness. If you are polite to someone when making a request, for example, then you allow the hearer to 'save face' when they turn down your request. Here is an example. John says:

> *Lend us twenty quid till tomorrow, Peter.*

What does Peter say? Peter 'loses face' whatever he says. If he says *No*, he loses face by refusing the request. If he says *Yes*, he loses face by seeming too cowardly to turn down John's brash request.

If John had said something like:

> *I'm really sorry, Peter, I'm in a bit of a pickle. You couldn't lend me twenty quid till the morning, could you? I collect my wages at nine o'clock.*

Then Peter could have said *No* by coming up with a polite refusal of his own. On the other hand, he could have appeared generous by agreeing to John's request. Either way, Peter would not have lost face. In addition, John could have saved his own face by being respectful and tactful.

So, rudeness is often 'face-threatening'. There are other ways in which face is threatened, or face is lost. You can *drop a brick/clanger, commit a gaffe* or *make a faux pas*. If you do this unintentionally, you may be considered *naïve, tactless* or *gauche*. You may have to try to remedy the situation in order to 'save face'. However, if you are deliberately *tactless*, you may be called *bitchy, catty* (Why are these terms female oriented?), *vindictive, cruel* or *arrogant*.

Finally, it may be necessary to be *impolite* when the situation is urgent:

> *Get me a bloody ambulance.*

and not

> *I don't suppose I could trouble you to telephone a paramedic team from the nearest hospital, could I?*

ACTIVITY 52

1 Turn these exponents of polite requests into complete sentences. Then put them in order of politeness. Think about the people you would use these requests with.

Alright if I …?
D'you mind if I …?
I hope you don't mind, but would it be at all possible for me to …?
I thought I might …
I wonder if I could possibly …?
I'd like to …
I'm going to …
Is it alright if I …?
Would it be alright if I …?
Would you mind if I …?

2 Go through the requests that you have just looked at. What differences are there in terms of (a) the hearer's power over the speaker, (b) the familiarity of the speaker with the hearer and (c) the ability of the hearer to carry out the request made by the speaker? How do you think these things affect politeness in general?

5.4 Taking turns in the conversation

It is very easy to gather conversation; you just tape record it. However, it is more difficult to record it 'naturally', so that people aren't self-conscious about speaking in front of the tape recorder. In addition, there are some problems with writing it down. For example, how do you show that people are speaking at the same time? However, it is estimated that in ordinary conversation, people 'overlap' in the conversation only for 5% or less of the time. How do you show how long the pauses are in a conversation? Do you show the little noises – *um, ah, mm, uh-ha*, and so on – that people make during a conversation? These noises, by the way, are called **back-channelling**.

More importantly, there are problems with actually *analysing* conversation. In previous chapters, you have seen that the organisation of pieces of text can follow certain rules. You have seen that there are certain things that make a text coherent. You have noted, in the list of differences between speech and writing, that writing tends to be controlled by one person at a time. A piece of written text can be 'rewritten' by another person; usually, but not always, working with the first writer. But written text needs to be 'coherent' for its message to come across. In speech, people speak to the needs of the moment. Most importantly, a conversation only exists when the second person has responded to the first person. And there are only a limited number of ways of predicting what that response might be.

This difference can be summed up by saying that analysis of written text may help you to become a better writer. That is one reason for the writing activities in this book. However, analysis of conversation is very unlikely to make you a better conversationalist.

Nevertheless, because conversation is a shared experience we can say a number of things about it.

As we have said, overlap in conversation is quite rare. This is because people are experts at **turn-taking**. When one person speaks, the other people are, mostly, quiet and wait their turn – as in this example, in which Eliška and James are talking about a summer visit to Eliška's grandparents in the Czech Republic. Eliška had not been there for two years:

> *James: We just went into the cottage. Like, she's not been there, for how many years?*
> *Eliška: For about two.*
> *James: Two years, and we just went in with this plastic bag. Emptied all the drawers of this completely useless memorabilia.*

Here, James is *holding the floor*; he then invites Eliška to answer a question. He ends his turn and invites Eliška to speak. James then carries on the story.

The next question is: 'How does James know when he can speak again?' The simple answer is that Eliška has replied to his question. But Eliška might have wanted to say more, to elaborate on the answer. How does James know that she didn't?

When we come to the end of a 'spoken thought', in English, our voice usually drops: the pitch of what we are saying usually falls. This fall in pitch is almost like a 'spoken full stop'. It tends to suggest to the others in the conversation that they can begin to speak. Other visual signals have been suggested for the ends of turns. One piece of research has suggested that children end their turns with movements of the head, down and to the left. Other research has suggested that listeners look steadily at the speaker while listening, with short times for looking away. Speakers will look at and turn away from the listener for equal periods of time. When speakers get towards the end of the turn, they will look for a longer time at the listener.

However, none of these things is really enough to indicate that a turn is coming to an end.

There is a rather cumbersome term for this moment: the 'transition relevance place', or **TRP**. At the TRP, the listener usually feels that he or she can *take over the floor*. The listener feels that it is the relevant moment for him or her to speak. If the listener can sense a TRP, but chooses not to take the turn, he or she can make one of the back-channelling noises that we have noted above. Look at this second extract from the same conversation (the square brackets here indicate overlapping speech):

> *Eliška: … And we were gonna go to the graveyard and see my, and see the graves of my grand, great-grandparents and that.*
> *James: We couldn't find them.*
> *Eliška: [We couldn't find them.*
> *James: We did find a small bird though there. [Yeah] I nearly stood on it and she was off looking for her, an, her, like, her grandparents' graves. And I was [Yeah], And I found this bird and I couldn't pick it up because it didn't like me.*

Note here that Eliška's second *Yeah* comes a split second after a TRP at the end of James' sentence.

Turn-taking in normal conversation is usually governed by whether or not people want to take advantage of the TRPs that they can sense. Either they take the floor or they don't. If they don't, then the first speaker is free to carry on talking.

Sometimes turns are part of a paired pattern.

If I say *Hello*, you say *Hello*: one greeting predicts another. If I say *Goodbye*, I don't expect you to say *Hello*. Groucho Marx sent up this expectation in his famous phrase *Hello, I must be going*. Other pairs like this include:

Apologising	Accepting the apology
Congratulating	Thanking
Offering information	Acknowledging the information.
Offering help	Accepting or rejecting help
Saying goodbye	Saying goodbye

It has also been suggested that the ringing of the telephone and the answering *Hello* are also a pair that fits in with other pairs of this kind. Note that these sequences remind us of the **functions** that we looked at above. This whole set is known as **adjacency pairs**. As that phrase suggests, an important point is that the two utterances in the sequence should be next to, or very near to, each other.

Adjacency pairs can be broken by what are called **insertion sequences** and **side sequences**. Look at these examples:

1   *A: May I have a bottle of Mich?*
    B: Are you twenty-one?
    A: No.
    B: No.

2   *A: What's the price now, eh, with VAT?*
    B: Er I'll just work that out for you.
    A: Thanks.
    B: Three pounds nineteen a tube, sir.
    [both adapted from S. Levinson, *Pragmatics*, Cambridge University Press, 1983]

In both cases, the first question is not answered until the second turn of the second person. In the first case, the answer is delayed because a question is asked of the first person. In the second case, the answer is delayed because the shop assistant can't give an immediate answer.

Sometimes speakers make a mistake. Look again at the first extract from the James/Eliška conversation. Notice how Eliška changes her words at the beginning of the extract:

> *Eliška: … And we were gonna go to the graveyard and see my, and see the graves of my grand, great-grandparents and that.*

Eliška makes a mistake, *grand*, and then repairs that mistake, *…great-grandparents*. In fact, it seems possible that she was on the verge of making the bigger mistake of suggesting that they were going to see her grandparents!

Later on in the same conversation, Eliška tries to find the right word for a Czech food:

> *Eliška: And then like little croissants but they weren't croissants, it's like little bread rolls they're really long. It's a Czech speciality.*

This self-correction is known as **self-repair**.

Repair can be used for other reasons as well. In the James/Eliška conversation, the interviewer could not hear one of the comments properly:

Eliška: We were investigating the upstairs little room because it has two floors, the country home. And the upstairs little room where I used to spend some time when I was a child. It's really nice. And it had this little drawer that all my things were in and it was really sweet. It was things passed on from my Dad like.
James: … which were tipped into a big plastic bag
Eliška: (big laugh) stolen
Interviewer: Plastic bag of what, sorry?

In this case, the interviewer needs a word, phrase or situation to be clarified. But the request for clarification could have come from any person in the conversation. This is known as **other-repair**.

ACTIVITY 53
What repairs are going on in these extracts?

1 *Jenny: And he gave a good*
   Harry: Very interesting
   Jenny: demonstration that students could actually <u>use</u>, saying that if you put your finger in the middle of your <u>mouth</u>, you could feel your <u>lips</u> coming forward and so on. The top line of that, er if you put your fingers at the <u>edge</u> of your mouth you could feel that your lips were contr<u>a</u>cting. And so on. As you went across the line. And if you touch your tongue or your neighbour's tongue
   Harry: (laughs) no that was a <u>JOKE</u>.

[courtesy of K. E. Richards]

2 *Eliška: …We bought loads of little things from stalls, and it's a*
   James: [It's this here
   Eliška: [little star on a necklace. He's only allowed to wear it when it's sunny, 'cos it's sun shaped. And.
   James: Got a cloud as well.
   Eliška: Got a cloud as well, so when it's cloudy he has to wear the cloud shaped necklace and when it's sunny, he has the sunshine. You see, it's a cunning plan. (laughs)
   James: Even though you said it was a star but that wouldn't make sense.

There is a fairly obvious difference between turns in a conversation that is free-flowing and a conversation that is controlled. Controlled conversations can happen in many situations: in law courts, at interviews and also on television in debates. In each of those situations, there is a 'chairperson' who gives out the turns, who selects the next speaker. In these controlled situations, the turns are often longer than in free-flowing situations.

Politicians are very good at extending their turns in debates. They do this in a number of ways. One way is to begin a turn with words such as *if* or *since*, which tell the listener that there are at least two clauses in the turn. For example:

If the government insists on its so-called ethical foreign policy, then there will be many people involved in the arms industries in this country who will lose their jobs.

or

However Mr Portillo defends his attacks on foreign students, he must always remember that they bring much needed money to a higher education system which the Tories systematically underfunded for years and years.

Another way of extending the turn is to introduce the turn by using one of the numbering devices that we looked at in Section 4.5. Another way is to pause when the sentence is obviously not complete. This means pausing at a word such as *but, and, however* or *because*.

ACTIVITY 54

Look at this excerpt from a politician's speech. Which of the devices mentioned above is this politician using to organise his speech?

> *Now I think one can see several major areas … there's first the question … now the second big area of course is the question of how you handle incomes and I myself very strongly believe that we have to establish in Britain two fundamental principles. First of all …*

> [Denis Healey, in M. Coulthard, *An Introduction to Discourse Analysis*, Longman, 1985]

In all of these situations, another speaker is clearly seen as interrupting if he or she attempts to break the flow of the first speaker.

5.4.1 Subjects

If these are the ways in which we organise the turns, how do we find things to talk about? We see and hear lots of things that seem newsworthy. But we have to choose carefully what we can talk about. People who talk all the time about nothing are bores. We also need to choose the right people to talk about the subject with. Most conversation seems to run on a 'need-to-know' basis. We can all think of things that we would not tell the person sitting next to us now. There might be other things that we could say to that person but which we would not say to others.

Good conversations seem to drift naturally from topic to topic. Sometimes this means thinking about how you will introduce a subject. If you introduce it too narrowly, often with an *I* at the beginning of the sentence, then the subject of the conversation might not be appealing enough.

If you say *I'm really sorry they threw Jackie off the course*, you may have said everything that is relevant to you, and left your partner in the conversation with very little way into the conversation. If you say *They're chucking someone else off the course*, then your partner has a way in.

Sometimes people fight to get their subject talked about.

▷ Who is fighting for which subject in this conversation?

> *Roger: Isn't the New Pike depressing?*
> *Ken: Hh. The Pike?*
> *Roger: Yeah! Oh the place is disgusting [Any day of the week*
> *Jim: [I think that P.O.P is*
> *   [depressing it's just –*
> *Roger: [But you go – you go – take –*
> *Jim: Those guys are losing money.*
> *Roger: But you go down — dow. down to the New Pikes there is a buncha people, oh, and they're old and they're pretending they're having fun, but really they're not.*

Ken: How c'n you tell? Mm?
Roger: They're – they're trying to make a living, but the place is on the decline,
's like a de[generate place
Jim: [so's P.O.P

[Sacks (1967), in M. Coulthard *An Introduction to Discourse Analysis*, Longman, 1985]

Jim and Roger are connecting the things that they say with the things that they have said in their own previous turns in the conservation. They are listening to each other, but only to the things that they can use themselves, for their own subject.

5.5 Organising conversations

We have just seen that there is organisation of conversation at the level of the utterance and the turn. Is there organisation at a higher level than that?

It is clear that there is organisation in places where the speakers have particular roles. There is organisation in the speaking that takes place between teachers and pupils in classrooms. There is organisation in the conversation between doctors and patients. There is also organisation when speakers talk about events and put those events into a story. There is also organisation in telephone conversations. We will now examine those situations.

5.5.1 Speaking in classrooms

Note that this section is called 'Speaking in classrooms', rather than 'Conversation in classrooms'.

▷ When teachers and pupils/students in primary or secondary schools speak to each other in the classroom, is this a conversation?
▷ What is the relationship between the teacher and the pupil in the classroom? Is it an equal relationship?

Think about those things as we now look at classroom language.

First, teachers and pupils usually speak during a fixed period of time – a lesson. The teacher usually starts, or tries to start, the speech in the classroom. A teacher usually starts the lesson with one, or more, of a small set of starting words: *OK, well, right, now, good.*

This set of words is usually followed by another group of words that acts as a focus for the lesson, or for a particular part of the lesson. This group of words usually tells the pupils what they are going to do next. Look at these two examples of starting words followed by focuses:

Teacher: Well, today I thought we'd do three quizzes.

Teacher: Now then ... I've got some things here, too. Hands up. What's that, what is it?

The lesson, or part of the lesson, can also end in a very similar fashion. The teacher sums up what the pupils have been doing. He or she then often uses a framing word. This framing word may well be the same kind of framing word that was used to start that part of the lesson. Look at these two endings of parts of lessons:

> *Teacher: What we've just done, what we've just done is given some energy to this pen, now.*

> *Teacher: Yes, I cut wood with the axe. Right ... Now, then, I've got some more things here ...*

In the second extract, you can see that the teacher is moving on to another part of the lesson.

In Section 5.4, we saw that people usually take turns to speak. This is also true of teachers and pupils speaking in a lesson. But the pattern is not simply teacher–pupil–teacher–pupil, and so on.

ACTIVITY 55

Look at this excerpt of teacher–pupil talk. What major difference can you find between the speech pattern here and the turn-taking that we looked at above? Think in particular about the teacher's response to the pupil's reply. Why have I chosen to call the student 'Pupil' here?

> *Teacher: Those letters have special names. Do you know what it is? What is one name that we give to these letters, Paul?*
> *Pupil: Er, vowels.*
> *Teacher: They're vowels, aren't they?*
> *Teacher: Do you think you could say that sentence without having the vowels in it?*
>
> [J. Sinclair and M. Coulthard, *Towards an Analysis of Discourse*,
> Oxford University Press, 1975]

Teacher–pupil speech in the classroom is not simply a teacher speaks to pupil, pupil speaks to teacher pattern; in other words, teacher–pupil, teacher–pupil. It is more of a teacher–pupil–teacher, teacher–pupil–teacher pattern. Teacher asks, pupil answers and teacher comments before moving on.

We can see this more easily if the dialogue is laid out as a table:

Teacher	Pupil	Teacher
1 *Those letters have special names. Do you know what it is? What is one name that we give to these letters, Paul?*	*Er, vowels.*	*They're vowels, aren't they?*
2 *Do you think you could say that sentence without having the vowels in it?*		

ACTIVITY 56

1 Look at the turns in this table. What is happening here? What are the pupils'
non-verbal responses? What kind of school is this talk happening in?

Teacher	Pupil	Teacher
1 *And what do we call this thing? What's this a bit of? Yes.*	*A piece of metal*	*A piece of metal good boy.*
2 *Can you point to a piece of metal in this room anybody a piece of metal in this room.*	*[Non-verbal response]*	*Yes*
3 *You go and show me one David a piece of metal*	*[Non-verbal response]*	*Yes that's a piece of metal well done a team point you can have one*
4 *Will you show me a piece of metal*	*[Non-verbal response]*	*Yes the radiator that's a piece of metal.*
5 *Hands up. What's that what's that? Yes Cleveland.*	*Piece of wood.*	*Piece of wood good piece of wood.*
6 *Point to a piece of wood everyone, piece of wood anywhere.*	*[Non-verbal response]*	*Yes that's fine.*

[J. Sinclair and M. Coulthard, *Towards an Analysis of Discourse*,
Oxford University Press, 1975]

2 Ask a teacher if you can record the first five minutes of a lesson. Write out the
speech and analyse it using the information that you have just looked at. Does
it fall into the pattern that you have just seen?

Try to do the same in a primary school, a secondary school and in a sixth-form
lesson? How similar are the language patterns in each situation? Think about
the pupil–teacher relationship in each case. Does that relationship affect the
pattern?

3 Look at this extract from the play *Unman, Wittering and Zigo*, by Giles Cooper.
The play is set in an all-boys public school. John is the name of the teacher and
the boys are given their surnames.

Does the dialogue in this play conform to the patterns of classroom language
we have looked at above? Would it be any good as a play if was more realistic?

John.   ... Now then: McMorrow and Purdie's history of England, chapter nine.
(The class noisily get out their books and open them) *All right, all right.*
(Silence) *Has anyone read chapter nine?*
Terhew. Yes, sir.
John. Good ...er, Terhew. Perhaps you'd give us an outline of its contents.
Terhew. Me, sir, oh no, sir.
John. And why not?
Terhew. I haven't read it, sir.
John. You said you had.
Terhew. No, sir, you asked if anyone had read it and I said yes, sir, Cuthbun has.

Bungabine. He's read the lot, sir.
Trindle. The whole book.
Cuthbun. It ends with the General Strike.
John. Does it? Well, tell us about chapter nine.
Cuthbun. Actually, sir, I left that chapter out. Terhew was wrong.
Terhew. I'm most terribly sorry, sir.
John. Shut up, Terhew.
Terhew. But I am, sir, really.

[Giles Cooper, *Unman, Wittering and Zigo*, Macmillan, 1971]

Do you think that John is having a good lesson with this class? In the light of what we have said about speech patterns in the classroom, can you say why John is having such a bad time with this class?

4   Look at these two three-turn sequences. Read them out loud, either to yourself or with a friend. What kind of tone emerges from the conversation? What does this tell you about three-turn sequences and power?

Mother: *have you brushed your teeth yet?*
Child: *yes*
Mother: *no you haven't*

Between two adults:

A: *what time did you come in last night?*
B: *about midnight?*
A: *no you didn't.*

[M. Coulthard and M. Montgomery (eds), *Studies in Discourse Analysis*,
Routledge and Kegan Paul, 1981]

5.5.2 Speaking to the doctor

We have looked at one situation that is quite tightly structured – the classroom. Another conversation situation that is structured for the speakers takes place in the doctor's surgery.

ACTIVITY 57

Think about the functions that a doctor must perform when having a consultation with a patient. What differences do you think there might be between consultations in a hospital and consultations in a G.P.'s surgery?

   Write down a list of functions. Now compare your list with these suggestions. They are in the order they might take place in during the consultation:

1   Greeting
2   Information extracting
3   Examination
4   Diagnosis
5   Predictions for the illness, and a cure
6   Leave-taking

Here are some suggestions for the language used by the doctor to perform these functions:

1   Greeting

Hello
Good morning
Mrs Jones?

2   Information extracting

What can I do for you today?
Can you tell me what happened?
Do you remember if your weight was on the foot?

3   Examination

Does it hurt here?
Can you bend it?
Can you just lie down a moment?'

4   Diagnosis

You haven't broken anything.
Yes, I'm afraid it's broken just here.

5   Predictions for the illness, and a cure

It should heal up quite quickly.
Take plenty of rest.
So we'll give you some ointment to apply three times a day.

6   Leave-taking

Bye-bye Mr Clarke.
Good, see you next week, then.
Right, thank you.

[adapted from C. Candlin *et al.*, in L. Selinker *et al.* (eds),
English for Academic and Specific Purposes, Newbury House, 1981]

Those are all the doctor's comments. What do you think the patients would be saying, either as their first turns or in reply to the doctor's utterances?

ACTIVITY 58

1   You have just seen the usual pattern of doctor–patient consultations. Now look at the following examples of doctor–patient interactions. Where in the pattern of consultations do they come? Do individual utterances fit into the pattern in different places? What are the patients doing at these points in the consultation?

   a   *Patient: It were just an old biro.*
   Doctor: Really …
   Patient: I was just bored in the lesson and was playing with it.
   Doctor: Uh-uh
   Patient: … it was only an old biro.
   Doctor: So…
   Patient: As I opened it the spring shot out.

b *Patient: Thank you.*
Doctor: Thank you
Patient: Thank you very much. I don't need to come any more.
Doctor: No need to come again unless you're worried.
Patient: All right, all right.

c *Doctor: You'll feel a bit sore. I don't think you've broken any bones or*
anything, but it might be a bit more sore tomorrow than it is today.
Patient: Yeah.
Doctor: Now if anything odd turns up come and see us, but if you're quite
happy, then, er, let nature do the job. Bye-bye Mr. Clark
Patient: Goodbye.

[C. Candlin *et al.*, op. cit.]

d *Doctor: Were you given the course of antibiotics?*
Patient: No, I was just given that pink, this pink watery stuff.
Doctor: Right, well, you need the, it should be treated and that's why you're not
better.

e *Doctor: Okay, I think what you have is, you have probably bruised your ribs and*
they can be quite painful and can take a while for it to get right again
Patient: Yes
Doctor: So, don't worry about it but give it time.
Patient: Yes.

[*The Surgery*, Channel Four Television]

2 Now look at these longer extracts. Where in the consultation do you think
these extracts come? What is the doctor doing with his repeated short words?

a *Doctor: Do you want to tell me what the problem is?*
Patient: I've got a terrible pain in me back.
Doctor: Mm-hm.
Patient: It's been coming on for the last month, Okay, getting worse every day
Doctor: Mm-hm, Yeah
Patient: I can't move, I can't get up

b *Doctor: Do you know what a brain scan involves?*
Patient: Yes, I've had two.
Doctor: Right, right.
Patient: Yes.
Doctor: But you were wondering why you'd been sent for another one.
Patient: Yes.
Doctor: Right. I think it's the only way we can monitor what's happening with the
aneurism, really
Patient: [That's right
Doctor: [What's happening is that that aneurism is pressing on the, the, the
particular nerve and making the eye turn outwards.
Patient: Mm-hm yes
Doctor: Do you notice any difference, I mean have you noticed anything
happening to you different?
Patient: Er, a month last Saturday I fell down the stairs.
Doctor: Oh dear

Patient: Now I came down two steps. And I changed my mind. And my balance isn't very good.
Doctor: Right
Patient: So, Oo, I had my balance checked at neurology.
Doctor: That's right
Patient: And they said it wasn't very good either.
Doctor: Mm
Patient: And they sent me to emergency.
Doctor: Right
Patient: And there were no bones broken but
Doctor: Right
Patient: Er, I had terrible pains in my er,
Doctor: Your tummy, yup.
Patient: Er, across my chest and my back.

[*The Surgery*, Channel Four Television]

3   You have just looked at two particular 'occupational varieties' of conversation. What do teacher–pupil and doctor–patient situations have in common? Are there any similarities in the positions that teachers and doctors have in society? Are there any similarities in the patterns of the conversations?

4   Think of other situations in which there are likely to be patterns in conversations. Think, first, of places where people have conversations of particular kinds; at the dentist's (see Section 4.6); at a restaurant; in a shop (particularly for electrical goods, or shops for goods where a lot of conversation with the assistants is involved – this might include shoe shops and jewellers) Write down what you think the pattern of the conversation might be. Then go out and record the conversation in the situation. You should always make sure, however, that you have asked the permission of anyone whose conversation you want to record. Do your predictions for the situation match the reality? In what ways do they differ?

5.5.3 Speaking on the telephone

Another area where there is evidence of organisation in conversation is on the telephone.

▷ What is the usual pattern of conversation at the beginnings of telephone calls?

The usual pattern can be shown like this.

Caller:	*(causes the phone to ring)*
Receiver (T1):	*Hello.*
C (T2):	*Hi, Phil.*
R (T3):	*Oh, hi, Anne.*

When Phil greets Anne twice, *Hello* and *hi*, is he *really* greeting Anne with Turn 1? No, he is answering the telephone. So, does Phil say hello to the telephone? Obviously not, but is he saying *Hello* to Anne? At this stage, he doesn't know who is calling, so he isn't saying *Hello* to anybody in particular yet.

One way of solving this puzzle is by suggesting that the ringing of the telephone is a *summons* and that T1 is an *answer* to that summons. So here we have another adjacency pair. When no one answers, then the T2 is, effectively, 'I can't respond to your summons'. This also helps to explain why the caller is likely to speak first if the receiver doesn't say anything when he or she picks up the phone. If the receiver doesn't speak, then the caller will usually repeat the summons.

Next there is T2. How does Anne know what to say to Phil? She knows because she recognises his voice. Therefore T1 has another function; it tells the caller that the receiver is the right person.

▷ If the receiver isn't the right person, what will the caller say?
▷ What usually happens after the 'real' greetings part of the conversation?

There at least two possibilities. The first possibility is that either the caller or the receiver will say something like *How are you?* or *How are things?* And the receiver or the caller will reply to the inquiry about his or her health. The second possibility is that the caller will give a reason for the call. Alternatively, these two possibilities may be combined.

1   *A: Hello there.*
     B: Hello.
     A: What's new with you?
     B: Not much, and you?
     A: Nothing.

           [M. Coulthard, *An Introduction to Discourse Analysis*, Longman, 1983]

2   *R: Hello.*
     C: Hello Rob. This is Laurie. How's everything.
     R: Pretty good. How 'bout you.
     C: Jus' fine. The reason I called was ta ask …

           [adapted from S. Levinson, *Pragmatics*, Cambridge University Press, 1983]

This first reason for calling is likely to be seen as 'privileged' and is likely to be referred to when the call comes to an end. Following on from the beginning of the call, the conversation usually flows in the ways that we have seen above.

As I'm sure we all recognise, ending telephone calls is quite a delicate business. We can do a number of things. First, we can make sure that the **subject** of the conversation at that moment has finished. A speaker can show he or she has very little extra to say on the subject by saying *all right, okay, so, well.* These are often pronounced in a rather exaggerated way, by lengthening the word, and by letting the intonation fall.

At this point, the other person can take up a new subject. The other person may just use that opportunity to close the conversation. The second person now has turned the first person's *well*'s and *okay*'s into a **possible pre-closing**. This is then followed by a **pre-closing sequence**. A pre-closing sequence may also contain other 'reasons' for stopping the conversation, such as

   Sorry, Kate, must go, there's someone at the back door.
   I gotta go. Ben's just come in crying.

These may happen, of course, when the receiver has run out of things to say, or cannot find a way to close the conversation naturally.

Alternatively, one speaker may offer the other the chance to stop:

Well, I'll let you get back to the box.
Well dear, I don't want to run up your phone bill.

Then, finally, there is the closing sequence of leave-takings, as we have seen before.

Look at this telephone ending, which follows the pattern that we have just examined:

End of subject	**Theresa**	*Yeah, well. Things uh always work out for the [best.*
	Dorinne	[Oh
		certainly
Pre-closing	**Dorinne**	*Alright Tess*
sequence	**Theresa**	*uh huh, Okay*
Closing sequence	**Dorinne**	*G'bye*
	Theresa	*Goodnight*

[M. Coulthard, *An Introduction to Discourse Analysis*, Longman, 1985]

ACTIVITY 59

Look at the following beginning and ending of a telephone conversation. How closely does it follow the pattern we have looked at above?

Phone rings
A: Hello
B: Hello
A: Oh hold on I've got to get the extension hold on
B: (silent)
A: Hello? Hello?
B: Yeah hello
A: Hello? Oh no we were just leaving actually
B: Oh why did you wake up late today
A: Yeah pretty late
B: Oh dear
A: So I've got to get him off to school. How are you anyway Danny?
B: All right
A: You all right
B: Uh-huh
A: Yeah?
B: Mm
A: You got home all right? You weren't too tired?
B: Well er, I got up pretty late myself I mean I – I was supposed to get up at about seven o'clock

…
A: OK Danny I must go. Look I'll – can I talk to you later on this morning?
B: Yeah OK sure
A: Is that OK Huh?
B: Sorry what was that
A: Can I – I'll talk to you when I get there
B: Yeah

> *A: I must go now*
> *B: OK*
> *A: Bye-bye*
> *B: Well have a nice day*
> *A: Thank you Bye-bye*
> *B: Bye*

[adapted from G. Francis and S. Hutton, in M. Coulthard (ed.), *Advances in Spoken Discourse Analysis*, Routledge, 1992]

5.5.4 Telling stories

We will now look at one final area of organised conversation; telling stories. We all tell stories and we would all like to be good at telling stories. But some people are much better at it than others. In this section we will look at the telling of stories by pairs of people. This kind of conversational pattern is often seen in television programmes such as *Blind Date*. In part of this TV show, two people tell the show's hostess about the holiday that they won on the programme in the previous week.

Oral stories often follow a six-part pattern:

- **Abstract (Ab.)**: What, in a nutshell, is this story about?

  Well, I must tell you what I've just heard.
  I think I've just had the most embarrassing moment of my life.

- **Orientation (Or.)**: Who, when, where, what?

  (In reply to the suggestion to tell 'something that Calvin did that was really wild')

  It was on a Sunday and we didn't have nothing to do after I – after we came from church.

  [W. Labov, *Language in the Inner City*, University of Pennsylvania Press, 1972]

- **Action (Ac.)**: Then what happened?

  And then the cat got it's paw stuck in the letter box.

- **Evaluation (Ev.)**: So what? How is this interesting?

  It was cool.
  We really enjoyed it.

- **Result (Res.)**: What finally happened?

  I win the fight.

- **Bridge (Br.)**: That's it, I've finished and am 'bridging' back to the present situation.

  I've never trusted him since.

It is important to note that evaluation can take place throughout the story. Evaluation is a way of claiming that the story is worth telling. It can take a number of forms, such as directly telling the audience that the story is worth listening to: *It was quite an experience, Yeah it was amusing.* It can also be something inside the story, such as commenting strongly on the action – *Emptied all the drawers of this completely useless memorabilia … And now it's lying around your house doing nothing, isn't it?* – or putting in your own evaluation of the actions of the story or things in the story: *It's really nice. And it had this little drawer that all my things were in and it was really sweet.* In essence, evaluation is commentary on the action. Of course, this may take place at the same time as the action is being described.

This is the beginning of James and Eliška's story of one day on their trip to the Czech Republic. It has been annotated to show where their utterances fit into the above categories. Note that it is not always possible to put utterances into a single category:

> *Eliška: Well, we set off in the morning. (Ab. & Or.) Reluctantly. (Ev.) (laughs) (Ev.)*
> *James: With a hangover (Or. & Ev.)*
> *Eliška: (laughs) (Ev.) with a hangover. Um. We headed towards the country house, via two buses and some metro. And we got the bus, we got there, greeted my grandparents, (Ac.) got attacked by a sheep-like dog called Jimmy. (Ac. & Ev.)*
> *James: The dog Jimmy. It was a scary little creature.'s about a thousand years old. (Ev.)*
>   *[It just doesn't, it just wobbles around*
> *Eliška: [It belongs to my grandparents. (laughs) And it's a bit old, like my*
>   *grandparents. [And it doesn't get a lot of disciplining (Ev.)*
> *James: [And it was raining when we got there. Was it raining when we*
> *got there? (Ac.)*
> *Eliška: Yeah it was (Ac.) and it got worse so (Ev.) And we were gonna go to the graveyard and see my, and see the graves of my grand, great-grandparents and that. (Ac.)*
> *James: We couldn't find [them (Ev.)*
> *Eliška: [We couldn't find them (Ev.)*
> *James: We did find this little bird though there. (Ac.)*
> *Eliška: Yeah (Ev.)*
> *James: I nearly stood on it and she was off looking for her, an, her, like, grand-parents' graves. (Ac. & Ev.) And I was*
> *Eliška: Yeah (Ev.)*
> *James: And I found this bird (Ac.) and I couldn't pick it up because it didn't like me. (Ev.)*
> *Eliška: Yeah, it didn't [like him. (Ev.)*
> *James: [And you came along. (Ac.)*
> *Eliška: And it sat on my arm (Ac.)*
> *James: Being all Snow White and Mary Poppins sort of thing. (Ev.)*
> *Eliška: And it actually leaped, jumped up my arm and sat there and looked at me, and was real sweet. (Ac. & Ev.) But we had to take it back because my grandparents didn't like it. (Res.)*
> *James: We took it to the cottage and the dog tried to eat it. And we just got it warm a little because it was soaking wet. (Ac.) It was only a baby. I think it had probably fallen out of the nest. (Ev.)*

Notice that the abstract and the orientation are together here. Also note that Eliška attempts to end the story. However, James sees that the link in events is missing. His final turn fills in the events between the bird's leaping up Eliška's arm and finally taking the bird back to where it was found. In addition, in this example there is no bridge back into normal discussion.

ACTIVITY 60

1 Look at this example of a story told by one person. Using the terms outlined above, decide how the story fits into the patterns given to you above:

> *(What was the most important fight you remember, one that sticks in your mind ...)*
> *Well, one (I think) was with a girl.*
>
>> *Like I was a kid you know,*
>> *And she was the baddest girl, the baddest girl in the neighbourhood.*
>> *If you didn't bring her candy to school,*
>>> *She would punch you in the mouth:*
>> *And you had to kiss her*
>>> *When she'd tell you.*
>> *This girl was only about 12 years old, man,*
>> *But she was a killer.*
>> *She didn't take no junk;*
>> *She whupped all her brothers.*
>> *And I came to school one day*
>> *And I didn't have no money.*
>> *My ma wouldn't give me no money.*
>> *And I played hookies one day.*
>> *(She) put something on me.**
>> *I played hookies, man,*
>> *So I said, you know I'm not gonna play hookies no more*
>> *'cause I don't wanna get a whupping.*
>> *So I go to school*
>> *And this girl says, 'Where's the candy?'*
>> *I said, 'I don't have it.'*
>> *She says, powww!*
>> *So I says to myself, 'There's gonna be times my mother won't give me money*
>> *Because we're a poor family*
>> *And I can't take this all, you know, every time she don't give me any money.'*
>> *So I say, 'Well, I just gotta fight this girl.*
>> *She gonna hafta whup me.*
>> *I hope she don't whup me.'*
>> *And I hit the girl: powwww!*
>> *And I put something on it.*
>> *I win the fight.*
>> *That was one of the most important.*
>
> ** To put something on someone means to 'hit him hard'.*

> [W. Labov, *Language in the Inner City*,
> University of Pennsylvania Press, 1972]

2 Tape record two friends talking about a shared experience, particularly an experience which has an element of story attached to it. Transcribe the part of the tape that concerns the story itself and examine it to search out the patterns that we have just looked at.

Glossary

This glossary contains details of the terms that are highlighted in **<u>bold underlined</u>** type in the text.

adjacency pairs   Sequences in conversations in which one utterance depends upon another utterance. For example, *hello* is normally followed by *hello*; *goodbye* is normally followed by *goodbye*; and *congratulations* is normally followed by *thank you*. (Section 5.4)

anaphoric reference   The kind of reference that is 'backward-looking'. (Section 2.1)

cardinal   A 'whole number' such as *one, two, three, four*, and so on. (Section 2.3)

cataphoric reference   The kind of reference that is 'forward-looking'. (Section 2.1)

clause   A group of words that contains a subject and a finite verb. For example, in *I bought that book <u>which was reviewed in the Sunday paper</u>*, the passage *which was reviewed in the Sunday paper* is a clause, because the verb group *was reviewed* has as its subject *which*. (Section 2.3)

coherence   The relationships between the *meanings* of utterances in speech, or of sentences in a written text. (Section 1.2)

cohesion   The grammatical and lexical devices that hold a text together; for example, pronouns, connectives and repetition of words. (Section 1.2)

co-hyponym   A member of a group of similar items within the domain of a **superordinate**. For example, *chair, table, chest of drawers* and so on are all items of furniture. *Furniture* is the superordinate, and *chair, table* and *chest of drawers* are all co-hyponyms of each other under the superordinate *furniture*. For further details, *see* **hyponymy** (Section 3.4)

collocation   The mutual attraction of words. If two words are collocates, then there is a greater than chance likelihood of them both occurring; for example, *dark* and *night*. (Sections 2.2, 3.6)

conversational implicature   The way in which speakers use the maxims of conversation to imply meaning. (Section 5.2)

co-operative principle   The implicit agreement between speakers to co-operate in a conversation so that communication is successful. (Section 5.2)

deictic   This refers to those things in the language which relate an utterance or sentence to time, space or person, for example, *now/then, here/there, his, hers*, and so on. From the Greek for 'pointing'. (Section 2.3)

dialogue   This is usually seen as the conversational interaction of two people. (Section 1.2)

discourse   In this book, the word 'discourse' is used to describe examples of both written and spoken language use. Others choose to use 'discourse' to apply to spoken language and 'text' to apply to written language. More specifically, in this book the term 'discourse' is used to describe the process by which a 'text' comes into being. (Section 1.2)

ellipsis   The leaving out of part of an utterance or sentence because they have already been mentioned and are, therefore, readily understood by the listener or reader. (Section 2.3)

exophoric reference   Usually where reference is made to the situation in which the discourse is happening; *see also* **anaphoric reference** and **cataphoric reference**, which are usually text only, or 'endophoric', reference. (Section 2.1)

exponent   The language of a **function**. For example, an apology may be delivered in several ways depending on the formality of the social context: (i) *Sorry, John*; (ii) *I'm very sorry about all that, John*; (iii) *I do apologize about all of that, John*. (Section 5.2)

finite verb   A form of a verb that has a subject and that shows past, present or future tense; for example, *I ordered, you ordered*; *I will order, you will order*. Non-finite verbs would include the infinitive *order*, or the participle *ordering*. (Section 2.3)

formality   This refers to the way in which the style or tone of writing or speech varies from casual to formal according to the situation, the person being spoken or written to, the place, the subject, and so on. (Section 3.7)

function   Language is seen to have many functions or purposes in communication; for example, *persuading, informing, arguing, describing, entertaining*. In addition, a group of words, such as a sentence or an utterance, may itself have a number of social functions; for example, *apologising, interrupting, asking for clarification, offering, refusing*, and so on. (Section 5.1)

genre   This is often used as a synonym for **register**. However, it may be defined more narrowly as being the discourses produced by a particular group in a particular situation. Common examples are *prayers, sermons, hymns, radio phone-in's*, and so on. There has been some effort to distinguish between 'simple' genres and 'complex' genres: a common example of the latter is *church service*, which includes the distinct genres of *prayer, sermon, hymn, eulogy*, and so on. (Section 3.7)

grammar   The study of the characteristic structures of words, phrases, clauses and sentences, that give the rules of the language; *see also* **syntax**. (Section 1.1)

grammarian   A person who studies, teaches, or writes about grammar. (Section 2.3)

hyponym, hyponymy   The relationship between two words where the meaning of one word is included in the meaning of the other, for example *furniture* and *chair*. *Furniture* is the general term, or **superordinate**, and *chair* is the **hyponym**. A chair is a piece of furniture. We can extend this to other items which are pieces of furniture, such as *table, chest of drawers, settee* and so on. In this case *chair, table, chest of drawers* and *settee* are all **co-hyponyms**. This kind of relationship can be layered: *furniture* is the superordinate of *chair* and *chair* is the hyponym of *furniture*. In turn *chair* is the superordinate of *armchair, swivel chair, rocking chair, deck chair*, and so on. (Section 3.4)

linguist   A person who studies or teaches linguistics. (Section 2.3)

maxim   A convention of spoken **discourse** relating to the quality, quantity, manner and relevance of what is said. (Section 5.2)

meronym   Also known as **part–whole**. This is an item that is part of a larger unit. Therefore, *spoke, hub, rim, tyre* are all parts of *wheel*. This relationship can be layered, because *wheel* is part of *bicycle*, as are *handle bars, frame, brakes, gears* and so on. (Section 3.4)

modal auxiliary verb   A member of a subclass of auxiliary verbs, including *may/might, can/could, shall/should, will/would* and *must*, used to show possibility, certainty, permission, obligation, ability, and so on. (Section 2.2)

ordinal   A numerical ranking or ordering, such as *first, second, third*, and so on. (Section 2.3)

part–whole   See **meronym**. (Section 3.4)

performative verb   A member of a group of verbs that 'do' things when they are uttered, for example, *dare* (*I dare you to jump in the deep end*), *swear* (*I swear I'll bring it back tomorrow, promise* (*I promise I'll be there*). Often, these words are formal and are used in formal situations: *There being no other business, I now declare this meeting closed*. (Section 5.1)

personal reference   Personal pronouns, possessives and personal adjectives, such as: *I, she, theirs, its, our*. (Section 2.1)

phrase   A small group of words that forms a grammatical unit but that does not contain a verb with a subject; for example, *all your complaints, into the darkness, working in the early hours*. (Section 1.1)

reference   (i) What words stand for in the world of our experience (see **referent**). (ii) What some words, particularly pronouns and comparatives, 'point to' in a text. *See also* **anaphoric reference, cataphoric reference, exophoric reference, personal reference**. (Section 2.1)

referent   (i) The real-world object that is described by a word. For example, the referent of the word *refrigerator* is the real object known as the refrigerator. (ii) The item that a pronoun or comparative points to in a text. For example, consider *The teacher gathered the children around. They all looked very excited*. In this example, *the children* in the first sentence is the referent of *They* in the second sentence.

register   A language variety used by a particular group of people who usually have the same occupation or area of occupation; for example, (i) doctors, nurses and health administrators, or (ii) lawyers, legal secretaries and solicitors. One register is usually different from another because of its use of a number of special words, or because it uses certain words or phrases in a special way; for example, *valve, clutch, body, spark-plug*, and so on. (Section 3.2)

repair   In conversation, the way in which mistakes and misunderstandings can be corrected by the speaker or others. Repair that is corrected by the speaker – by him- or herself – is called 'self-repair'. Repair that is corrected by others is called 'other-repair'. (Section 5.4)

superordinate   A general term for a group of items. For further details, *see* **hyponymy** (Section 3.4)

synonym   A word that means substantially the same as another; for example, *owner* and *possessor*. (Sections 2.4, 3.2)

syntax   (The study of) the structure of sentences. (Section 1.1)

text   A sequence of sentences or utterances marked by **cohesion** and **coherence**; *see also* **discourse**. (Section 1.0)

turn-taking   The way speakers behave in conversation; in particular, the way a listener knows when he or she can take a turn and speak in the conversation. (Section 5.4)